It's not who we are underneath..............it's what we _do_ that matters.

Cape - Diem

Chapter One

He who returns from a journey is not the same as he who left

Chapter Two

Learning is a treasure that will follow its owner everywhere

Chapter Three

Hand one – the slave

Chapter Four

Hand Five

Chapter Five

Hand Two

Chapter Six

Hand three

It's not who you are underneath...it's what you do that defines you.

Chapter Seven

Hand four

Chapter Eight

Hand of reality

www.lastingchange.uk

It's not who you are underneath...it's what you do that defines you.

360 –Degree Power Thoughts

I feel good about myself everyday.

It's not who you are underneath...it's what you do that defines you.

12 years Lost

Have good trust in yourself ... not in the One that you think you should be, but in the One that you are. Life isn't as serious as the mind makes it out to be.

It's not who you are underneath...it's what you do that defines you.

Chapter 1

"He who returns from a journey is not the same as he who left."

If you ask me now, I don't know why I did it. Losing two members of your immediate family in the same month didn't help. It messes with your head. Plus all the other stuff 20 years ago. It doesn't matter how mentally strong you think you are; everyone has their limits. Everyone!

So there I was, in the South China Sea, pitch black and desperately clinging to what was once a light aircraft's wing. The thing was, I had no idea what had happened or where I was. I kept passing out and waking up as the waves tossed my lifeless body around and around.

I was on my way to see a friend in India; I decided to get away from the stress and pressure, I just couldn't cope any more. The issue was I would never make it to India. As the waves took me under time after time I realised that I may never make it anywhere.

Desperate to survive, I took one last deep breath and braced myself for the onslaught of waves and debris that had battered my weak body for the past two hours. That's when I saw the light; I really did think it was time to meet my maker! It wasn't until sometime later I realised the light was my saviour. I found myself in the back of an open jeep bouncing around surrounded by an array of dark shadows speaking a language I didn't understand.

Doctors! I was safe.

360 –Degree Power Thoughts

I am willing to change; it is my right to be happy.

I was half right, I was safe but they were not doctors. I remember desperately trying to stay awake as we drove through thick woodland and dense forest tracks. Unfortunately, despite my efforts to stay awake, I just could not do it. The voices became more and more distant, my eyes heavy and I just had to sleep.

I would later find out I slept for 27 hours straight. The issue was, I had no idea where I was and even less of an idea who or what my rescuers' were? However, the smell was something that brought back memories. The smell of burning incense filled the air only to be equalled by the warm breeze seeping in through the open windows.

I was surprised by the light. Natural light, not the fake, replica light made by bulbs or energy saving gadgets. In truth there were no lights or light switches. As I slowly began to sit up I realised three things; first I hurt from head to toe, it was like being back in the ring after a fight, but having Mike Tyson as your opponent. Second, this was no hospital. Third, there were no plug sockets. I know that the lack of plug sockets may not be on your list of priorities when waking up after 27 hours. It's just, I was looking for my phone.

Everything seemed to be working, on me I mean. I slowly made my way to the light dragging my feet, desperately trying to stay upright. Finally, I made it to the large open window that gave way to a stone balcony. Two things became apparent; I was in a remote location with nothing but trees, fields and open country side. As far as the eye could see, nothing but a sea of green, beautiful sprawling landscape.

Second, the silence was deafening! Nothing, not a sound, except the hum of the birds. Where the hell am I?

At first, I said it in my head, "Where the hell am I?" over and over again. I must have said it out loud because a calm gentle voice said "Vietnam."

"You must have lots of questions, please follow me."

I was finding it difficult to see, not because I needed glasses to see correctly but rather my head was spinning.

A slim figure in orange, stood there waiting for me to follow.

"Where am I?" I said in a low broken voice.

He turned and pointed to a carving in the stone wall.

"He who returns from a journey is not the same as he who left."

"Follow me" he said in a soft voice, as he turned and walked down a long and straight corridor, with floor to ceiling marble slabs dusted with Buddha statues giving off that smoky aroma.

Eventually we entered the light. Outside in the bright sunshine the hum of the birds became sharp and clear. "Please wait" he said and then walked away. I have no idea how long passed but the sun had gone away, the birds were silent and the aroma gone.

"Welcome" said a strong but comforting voice. As I turned, I was offered a seat next to my companion.

"Where am I?" I croaked.

"You have many questions, I know. Allow me to explain"

Sitting there in the blue tint of the moon, my companion, who I would later address as Master Yip, explained only one person survived.

"13 people on that plane, one survivor, you! Why do you think that was?"

Images of chaos, confusion and madness filled my head as I recalled the disaster in slow motion, until a sudden jolt brought me back to the here and now.

"I don't know, I really don't know." With fear and confusion in my voice I struggled to continue.

"Tomorrow you will decide if you want to stay or go home. We can take you to the nearest town and you can continue your life as you always have." Master Yip continued, "You can go home and be the *victim* for everyone to admire, or you can stay here and leave when you are ready."

I don't think I understood. "Ready for what?"

"He who returns from a journey is not the same as he who left." Master Yip whispered.

"Your choice is simple, return as the *victim* or stay here until you are ready to return as the *victor*, the *champion* or the *enlightened one*. Your choice."

Before he left, he told me a story and then asked a question. He began.

A Japanese master received a university professor who came to enquire about Zen. The Japanese master served tea. He poured his visitor's cup full, and then kept on pouring. The professor watched the overflow until he no longer could restrain himself. 'It is over full, no more will go in!'

"Like this cup," said the Japanese master "you are full of your own ways and opinions. How can I show you true success unless you first empty your cup?" After a short pause the question came.

"My question to you is; what is the usefulness of a cup?"

The blank expression on my tired face must have struck a chord with Master Yip, as for the first time he raised a smile. "Think about it tonight as you sleep."

Walking back to my sun filled room only to find the pale moonlight had replaced the radiant beams, I began to read the scriptures and leanings carved into the stone walls. One spoke volumes to me.

Your teacher can open the door but you must enter by yourself.

It was clear I was free to leave in the morning knowing that my label as **Victim** and **sole survivor** would define who I was and who I would be for the rest of my life.

It's not who you are underneath...it's what you do that defines you.

360 –Degree Power Thoughts

I recognise the opportunities that are all around me.

I did try to sleep that night, but the only thing I could hear was master Yip's voice saying *"He who returns from a journey is not the same as he who left."*

What did that mean? Why did he ask about the usefulness of a cup?

The storm that brought me here created a storm within a storm! It wasn't the storm that brought down the plane that troubled me, no. It was the storm brewing inside me. That worried me. I was alive. Why? Why me? To most people the decision would be easy, GO HOME! I had an issue with what people call conformity, I always have had. Now I had a storm in a storm.

Morning came and I still hadn't slept, after 27 hours straight sleeping perhaps I would never sleep again?

"Have you figured it out yet?" As I turned, I realised Master Yip had been watching for some time. "Often one finds one's destiny just where one hides to avoid it." He said. Then he smiled and sat next to me.

"Have you figured it out yet?" He repeated.

"No," I replied with some degree of embarrassment.

"Good. Have you made your decision to stay or to go?"

"If I stay how will I know when it's time......................."

Master Yip interrupted "Only you will know when the time is right, perhaps when you have discovered the usefulness of a cup you can leave?"

"What will I do here?"

"Learn of course. There are many untold truths for you to share when you leave. I want you to tell the world, tell everyone the *truth*."

It's not who you are underneath…it's what you do that defines you.

360 –Degree Power Thoughts

I am unlimited in my own ability to create the future I want.

It's not who you are underneath...it's what you do that defines you.

Chapter 2

"Learning is a treasure that will follow its owner everywhere."

As I drove back from London to my home in the English countryside, I couldn't believe it had been 7 years since I arrived back from Vietnam. 7 years and so much had happened, well that was an understatement!

After the turmoil and whirlwind of the first six weeks back had died down. After the questions and quizzing from authorities and the public had been forgotten, I began to fulfil my destiny. I had spent twelve years 'lost'.

Lost, the headlines said;

12 years lost

In reality I had found myself, I was re-born.

Driving back I began to realise the enormity of what I had achieved in seven short years. I had accomplished what only 1% of the world's population could ever dream of.

Master Yip's words rang true in my head;

"Your choice is simple, return as the **victim** or stay here until you are ready to return as the **victor**, the **champion** or the **enlightened one**.

At first I was the victim with sympathy overload from everyone in every corner of the globe.

12 years lost taught me on defining phenomenon. *I learnt how to change two letters.* Before I tell you what they are you need to understand something. I spent twelve years of my life learning the *truth.*

Then I spent 7 years putting the *truth* into action, you know. Real life, not fantasy like so many "gurus" who jumped on the Law of Attraction gravy train, this really was a defining moment and a life changing phenomenon.

The person sat on that plane all those years ago was a very different person to the one you know now. Back then my name was AJ. I was recently bankrupt with no job. I lived in a rented flat above a shop in a busy high street. The only family I had was a sister who had her own problems.

It wasn't 12 years lost. It was 12 years of learning to **change two letters**. (Patience, you will discover them in your own time.) I remember the feeling of shock and the total incomprehensible **_trust_** of gripping onto the debris in the ocean that night.

The very same feelings and emotions engulfed me right now as I drove down the dark motorway. I had to pull into the services before I slammed my car into the central reservation. Taking a deep breath, I began to smile as I realised the feelings of shock were good feelings. I had just sold my Tec Company (OviTEC) to city investors for more than £2 billion. All the wealth I could ever want was now mine and the only reason for my new found wealth was learning how to **change two letters.**

Master Yip changed my name, he called me Ovi, I didn't know why then, but now I do. As I sat at the wheel of my luxury vehicle parked under the dim lights that surrounded the car park, I remembered the first story Master Yip ever told me. He had made me sit from sunrise to sunset looking at the sprawling and expansive countryside in silence. The moonlight hit the stone walls causing a vacuum of light to dance around the courtyard, reflecting the carvings along the stone walls.

360 –Degree Power Thoughts

I have many dreams and I know that I deserve to have them.

"What have you learnt today Ovi?" Master Yip asked.

"How to sit and be bored." Was my reply. That was the wrong thing to say, Master Yip made me do that for 30 days straight after that flippant remark.

"Have you heard about the traveller?" He asked.

"No"

"Then let me enlighten you" He continued;

As he walked, the traveller noticed a monk tending the ground in the fields beside the road. The monk said "Good day" to the traveller, and the traveller nodded to the monk. The traveller then turned to the monk and said, "Excuse me, do you mind if I ask you a question?"

"Not at all," replied the monk. "I am travelling from the village in the mountains to the village in the valley and I was wondering if you knew what it is like in the village in the valley?" "Tell me," said the monk "What was your experience of the village in the mountains?"

"Dreadful," replied the traveller, "to be honest I am glad to be away from there. I found the people most unwelcoming. When I first arrived I was greeted coldly. I was never made to feel part of the village no matter how hard I tried. The villagers keep very much to themselves; they don't take kindly to strangers. So tell me, what can I expect in the village in the valley?"

"I am sorry to tell you," said the monk "but I think your experience will be much the same there". The traveller hung his head despondently and walked on. A few months later another traveller was journeying down the same road and he also came upon the monk.

"Good day," said the traveller. "Good day" said the monk. "How are you?" asked the traveller. "I'm well," replied the monk, "Where are you going?"

"I'm going to the village in the valley," replied the traveller "Do you know what it is like?" "I do," replied the monk "But first tell me - where have you come from?"

"I've come from the village in the mountains."

"And how was that?"

"It was a wonderful experience. I would have stayed if I could but I am committed to travelling on. I felt as though I was a member of the family in the village. The elders gave me much advice, the children laughed and joked with me and people were generally kind and generous. I am sad to have left there. It will always hold special memories for me. And what of the village in the valley?" he asked again.

"I think you will find it much the same," replied the monk, "Good day to you".

"Good day and thank you" the traveller replied, smiled and journeyed on.

It's true, for 30 days from sunrise to sunset in rain and shine we sat there just looking. Yes I said we, Master Yip brought breakfast each morning and stayed until the sun had gone. We never spoke, we didn't need words. Each morning for 30 days was ground hog day; Master Yip would say the same things then sit with me in silence.

"Ovi. Your choice is simple, return as the **victim** or stay here until you are ready to return as the **victor**, the **champion** or the **enlightened one**." Then he said "You will know when it's time to leave, when you have **changed two letters**."

I was never any good at cryptic clues. "What letters? I haven't seen a postman!" Then we sat until sunset, the next day was the same and the next.

"Ovi. Your choice is simple, return as the **victim** or stay here until you are ready to return as the **victor**, the **champion** or the **enlightened one**." Then he said "You will know when it's time to leave when you have **changed two letters**."

"Have you found the **truth** yet Ovi?" asked master Yip on the final day of our 30 day meditation.

"Who's **truth?**" I replied

"Exactly." said Master Yip, and walked away.

I was brought back to reality, the here and now by the slamming of a car door as two young women ran into the services to get shelter from the rain.

In the weeks that followed and news became public about my new found wealth I received tens of thousands of letters and emails asking for help, mainly money, some marriage proposals.

I booked a train ticket for Friday back to my old town; it's good to do something different every now and then. I remembered the old gym that was under the arches. I used to watch from the side as each fighter went through a tough drill of exercise and fighting routine. I didn't have the money to join in, so I just sat watching. That's when Mick who ran the gym picked me up literally off my feet and made me train with the others. "I don't have any money" I said.

"I don't want your money" he said and walked off. At the end of the session I went to thank Mick but before I could say a word he said "Friday."

"Err no it's Wednesday." I said

"Be here Friday same time."

"I don't have any money."

"I don't want your money, be here Friday."

And that was that, every Wednesday and Friday we would train until he put me through my qualification and I became a coach for him.

Today was Friday; I picked up my train ticket from the station and set off. It was December so I wrapped up well and put my old woolly hat on, even I didn't recognise myself. I had packed an overnight bag with a few essentials in and I was on my way.

360 –Degree Power Thoughts

I take Positive Massive Action every day.

It was like going back 20 years, same sign on the door, same grunts and squeaks coming from inside. The only difference were the faces. I walked inside and up to the office door.

"Is Mick here?" I asked

"£2 per session and you will need your own gloves." came the reply.

"I'm not here to train; I wanted to talk to Mick." I said as the bell rang for the session to start.

"He's not here."

"Where can I find him?"

He eventually looked up from his desk and said "He passed away last year" He stood up and did a double take. "Welcome home AJ. Or is it Ovi? Mick talked about you. What are you doing here?"

That was a great question, I didn't know, maybe reminiscing or perhaps something more purposeful.

"Everything has changed AJ, I mean everything. The gangs have taken over, crime is just beyond belief but the worrying thing is knife crime. Every day another stabbing, I try my best here to keep them off the street but it's a drop in the ocean"

Tommy was old school, just like Mick, he had been training for the gym for years. I met him once, nice kid, I liked him.

I recognised some of the gym equipment, 20 years on and still the same worn out bags hanging up, the place looked tired, sad and in need of new gear.

"That's my address." said Tommy as he handed me a scrap of paper, "drop around about seven that's when we eat, you are welcome to join us."

I decided to book into a local hotel to rest and freshen up, I had been on the train for almost two hours I needed to shower and get ready.

As I arrived at Tommy's house later that evening one thing was obvious, he had a great family. Nothing was too much trouble. With Tommy Junior fast asleep, we sat in the lounge talking about Mick and his work in the local community. Tommy's wife Jasmine was great; she worked two jobs to help support the family. As did Tommy, he had a local retail shop in the village and then coached the fighters most evenings. Things were tough but they were making a living, getting by.

"I don't mean to pry." Tommy said "but how have you done it? You know success and all that, especially after the crash and everything."

Just before I could answer Jasmine cut Tommy's question short. "We agreed, not to ask about that, remember?"

"I know but............"

"But nothing" Jasmine stood up, she looked embarrassed.

I had to say something. "Please, sit it's OK. Honestly it's fine. In fact I haven't spoken about that part of my life to anyone."

"No I'm sorry AJ, I shouldn't have said anything" Tommy looked at me and spoke volumes without saying a word.

"He's got all their books" Jasmine said trying to change the subject.

"Who's books?" I enquired.

"You name them from Branson to Bronson and Trump to The Krays, he has them all. Here look"

She opened the cupboard under the stairs to reveal a library of super successful business and cultural figures.

"When's yours coming out?" Tommy asked.

"Ha-ha. No one would want to read about me" I joked.

"AJ, you are worth a fortune, you are in all the magazines and papers. You have more money than Sir Alan. You went missing 12 years. 12 years lost remember. You haven't told anybody what happened, something about amnesia? I think I would like a bit of memory loss if it brings me half of what you are worth."

"Can I ask you a question Tommy?" I said.

"Sure I didn't mean to speak out of term." was the nervous reply.

"Tommy, relax. You have the guts to ask what others won't. I really like you and your family. My question is, when you have finished a book, what do you do?"

"I put it back on the shelf, or I give it to someone who needs it"

"Correct, but also wrong" I said "I'm sorry but that's what everyone does" I added.

"OK, what should I do with them?"

After the short silence I decided to say the first thing that came into my head.

"Your choice is simple, return as the **victim** or stay here until you are ready to return as the **victor**, the **champion** or the **enlightened one**. You will know when it's time to leave when you have **changed two letters**."

"Where did that come from?" asked a confused Jasmine.

"Do you want to know? I mean really want to know what happened to me for 12 years."

As we sat in the lounge I had a feeling of excitement and trepidation, I had never talked about this to anyone.

"Listen." I said "It's late shall we do this tomorrow?"

360 –Degree Power Thoughts

I take time each day for my guided learning.

"What, you're joking! Tell, tell everything." They said in unison.

I brought them up to speed with the usefulness of a cup and my 30 day induction to meditation.

"You know, on the last day of meditation Master Yip asked me if I had found the **truth**."

"Who's **truth**?" Tommy said

"That's what I said to Master Yip, man that played on my mind for a long time, 12 years to be exact. I figured out the usefulness of a cup shortly after the meditation. Master Yip was getting me empty my mind, get rid of its contents. Shake off the past conditioning. That's why a cup is useful"

I did detect confusion from both Jasmine and Tommy.

"Let me demonstrate." I went into the kitchen and brought a cup full of water and a bottle of milk.

"Fill the cup with milk." I said.

"It's full." They both said.

I sat down and said nothing. I sat there and watched and listened. After a couple of minutes I added.............

"Ovi. Your choice is simple, return as the **victim** or stay here until you are ready to return as the **victor**, the **champion** or the **enlightened one**." Then he said "You will know when it's time to leave when you have **changed two letters**."

"Now I am really confused" Tommy said. "What letters? The postman has already been."

"Fill the cup with milk" I repeated

"It's full!"

"I Know; fill the cup with milk" I repeated for the second time.

Jasmine smiled. "Meditation, empty your mind. Tommy empty the water down the sink please" And then added "The usefulness of a cup is in its emptiness. As it is with the mind"

"Bingo well done." I replied.

"Thank you, but what is the *truth* and what letters need to change?" added Jasmine.

"Now that is a whole new ball game" I continued, "Changing two letters took me a lot longer, but in reality the answer was always there, in front of me, as it is with you." (And you the reader)

The *truth* wouldn't become clear for a long time, but when it did it changed everything, and I really mean everything.

I continued to tell Tommy and Jasmine about my leanings with Master Yip.

"Master Yip taught self-discovery. You cannot teach people, they can only discover the *truth*. I know what you are thinking, what *truth*, what is the *truth?* By the end of our time here I guarantee you will know the *truth*."

"Grab a pen and some paper" I said. "I am going to tell you the motto of Master Yip and the elders. These words were carved into the walls of the Great Hall. Write this down............" I instructed.

"The Truth is the only law that matters"

I then said "Write this down as well"

"Your choice is simple, return as the **victim** or stay here until you are ready to return as the **victor**, the **champion** or the **enlightened one**. You will know when it's time to leave when you have **changed two letters**. The **truth** will appear when you are ready"

So the motto was *"The Truth is the only law that matters"*

I didn't like rules or being told what to do, I thought I knew best, so being confronted with a **law** my rebellious nature was bound to surface at some point. And it did.

Carved beneath the motto was the **answer** to the **truth**.

Master Yip told me that everything I needed to find the **truth** was here.

"Your choice is simple, return as the **victim** or stay here until you are ready to return as the **victor**, the **champion** or the **enlightened one**. You will know when it's time to leave when you have **changed two letters**. The **truth** will appear when you are ready"

It was now 10PM so I suggested we carry this on tomorrow as I thought they had both hit their limit.

"You are not going anywhere!" exclaimed Jasmine. "I need to know what the **truth** is. Besides I could never get to sleep now, not after what you have started. If it takes all night and all day, you're staying!"

360 –Degree Power Thoughts

I keep my thoughts focused on goals every day.

It's not who you are underneath...it's what you do that defines you.

Chapter 3

Hand One
The Slave

"A man grows most tired while standing still."

Seven years back in the UK, £2 billion better off and yet I hadn't spoken to anyone about my 12 year absence; why? I have always been a private person I didn't post my daily routine on social media or tell the world what I had for breakfast. I went about my work and stayed low, off the radar, not drawing attention to myself.

What I was about to tell Tommy and Jasmine would break all my self-imposed rules of privacy. It needed to be told, not for the benefit of Tommy or Jasmine, no. For my benefit, I hadn't come to terms with what happened, I needed to tell someone.

The words of Master Yip had haunted me for seven years but I remember the conversation like it was yesterday..................

"What will I do here?"

"Learn of course, there are many untold truths for you to share when you leave. I want you to tell the world, tell everyone the truth."

"I need you to close your eyes and imagine what it was like for me in a place I didn't know" I said. "This place would be my home for many years, the place I found the *truth*. I will let you into a secret; I didn't have to travel to the other side of the world to find it. I had it with me all the time, and so it is with you" (And you)

Master Yip talked about the *elders,* the ones who built the monastery. He said to uncover the **truth** you have to respect, value and master the "**Seven Hands**"

The **Seven Hands** are a Chameleon, ever changing to master their surroundings. You must master each hand to find the **truth**.

"Can I ask a question?" Tommy said.

"Sure"

"What should I do with the books I have read?"

"That my friend is hand five, be patient and the Chameleon will reveal its **truth** colour."

"Can I ask you a question?" I continued "Have you any idea what two letters you and I need to change?" (I'm also asking you!)

"NO" Jasmine said; shaking her head.

"Let me tell you what Master Yip told me. **Two words, five letters both, each begin the same their ending not so**. You will know when it's time to leave when you have **changed two letters**. The **truth** will appear when you are ready"

"Your choice is simple, return as the **victim** or stay here until you are ready to return as the **victor**, the **champion** or the **enlightened one**."

I then sat and said nothing. After a short time I could see a realisation with Jasmine.

"You cannot teach people, they can only discover the **truth**." she said "Master Yip taught you that, and now you are doing the same. Tell me what Master Yip told you about the two words again please"

Two words, five letters both, each begin the same, their ending not so. You will know when it's time to leave when you have **changed two letters**. The **truth** will appear when you are ready"

"It's not about the postman is it? Tommy, where is that piece of paper with the motto on?"

"The Truth is the only law that matters"

"Your choice is simple, return as the *victim* or stay here until you are ready to return as the *victor*, the *champion* or the *enlightened one*. You will know when it's time to leave when you have *changed two letters*. The *truth* will appear when you are ready"

"Change two letters, change two letters! That's it change IM to OR."

"Well done"

Tommy was blank, he couldn't see it.

As Jasmine was just about to explain I stopped her. "Self discovery, Tommy has to see it for himself"

And that is why I am not telling you! If you haven't got it yet don't worry you will a little later, I promise.

"I still don't know about the truth" added Jasmine.

"I know. You will only discover that when the last hand has been played."

Tommy and Jasmine sat next to each other as I explained how "**The Salve**" helped me to understand my own behaviour.

I took them back to my first few months with Master Yip. The meditation taught me a valuable lesson.....the usefulness of a cup and an empty mind have so much in common.

"There are only three letters of the alphabet you need to remember when you are here Ovi" Master Yip looked at me and continued "ABC. This is the key to your past behaviour, and the first clue to the **truth**."

ABC was all that mattered to Master Yip, it became clear that it had made me who I was, and it has made you who you are.

Hidden away under the monastery was the wisdom space. This space was sacred and hallowed to everyone there; there were rules for those who were allowed to enter. You had to bring an empty cup, that was the most important thing, the second was to remember the motto and recite it before you entered.

"The Truth is the only law that matters"

The corridors that lead to the wisdom space were filled with the teachings of thousands of years. The elders had discovered the seven hands when they built the monastery, they were buried over 100 feet beneath the mountain; locked away in a stone tomb. Nine scrolls locked in a vault, the last resting place of the wealthy *Ovi dynasty.*

The *Ovi dynasty* was at one point in time the wealthiest family in the entire world. The *truth* kept them there for over 900 years. The Ovi Empire came to an end when the pandemic struck. Weeks before it wiped out millions of people the *Ovi dynasty* elders buried the scrolls deep in the mountain, they remained undiscovered until Master Yip's ancestors built the monastery and discovered the stone tomb.

Nine scrolls telling the entire story of the rise of the *Ovi dynasty.*

360 –Degree Power Thoughts

I feed my mind with knowledge every day; and act on the learning's every day.

A blueprint for both financial and worldly success; Master Yip's ancestors pieced the scrolls together to reveal exactly how the *Ovi dynasty* became the global dominant force for over 900 years. "And now you have the opportunity to take it to the world." Master Yip exclaimed.

As we sat in the learning space it became obvious that my physical wounds had healed, mentally I was broken, damaged and defeated. "Why now? Why share the secrets of the *Ovi dynasty* now? Why not years ago?"

Master Yip didn't say anything for a couple of minutes; he walked over to the first scroll that was still encased in its stone tomb. "Nine tombs and seven hands, seven lessons from the *Ovi dynasty* and two *encoded master messages*."

He placed the tomb with the scroll still inside on the stone bench next to me and said, "Two things are right. The person and the time." He opened the tomb and placed the rolled scroll into my hands. "You are the right person, that makes now the right time. You will share this with the world when you have proven they work. Now open the scroll."

It said. ***"The Truth is the only law that matters"***

"You already knew that, didn't you Ovi?"

"It's in the great hall." I said.

"No, before you came here you knew that."

"I didn't come here; you brought me in the back of a truck."

"Ovi, you have walked the grounds of this monastery. Have you seen a truck?"

"No"

"We have no truck. We have no need for a truck."

"Then how did I get here?"

"Only you know that" Master Yip continued. "We found you at the gates to the monastery."

Handing me the second scroll he invited me to open it. It said;

Your choice is simple, return as the *victim* or stay here until you are ready to return as the *victor*, the *champion* or the *enlightened one*. You will know when it's time to leave when you have *changed two letters*. The *truth* will appear when you are ready.

"Ovi, what is the *truth*?" asked Master Yip.

The truth was, I was further away from the *truth* now than I ever was.

"Time for meditation" Said Master Yip. "We will continue tomorrow."

The two encoded master messages had been given to me when I first arrived at the monastery. I didn't realise it at the time but Master Yip had started the ABC process, I was about to find out what the **slave hand** was, and why they were called **hands**.

Encoded massage one was;

"The Truth is the only law that matters"

The second was;

Your choice is simple, return as the **victim** or stay here until you are ready to return as the **victor**, the **champion** or the **enlightened one**. You will know when it's time to leave when you have **changed two letters**. The **truth** will appear when you are ready.

As I entered the learning zone with my empty cup I noticed a drawing on the slate wall. Think of the slate wall as a PowerPoint presentation, it was a visual way for Master Yip to get me to understand a learning point.

"What do you see Ovi?" asked Master Yip

"I see someone who is chained to a habit."

"I see you, chained to your past. A B C." Master Yip continued. "Let me explain why they are called hands. Each hand has five *realities* each working independently from each other, however each working towards a common goal."

"This is the first; it's called the *slave hand*. In the palm of that hand sits you. You are a *slave* to its five *realities*"

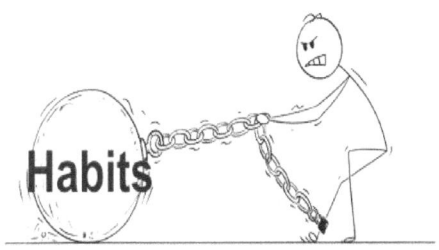

Truth number one is that your habits will define what you will become in later life. We (you) are a slave to your past learning and conditioning.

Reality two is the A B C. You must master this to move on to any other hand!

A – Always

B – Being

C – Conditioned

What does that mean? Conditioned simply means to learn or to train. The Ovi dynasty discovered that even in the womb babies can still learn. Children were at the heart of their beliefs. How you talk to and treat children, from zero to six years old would define who they would become for the rest of their lives.

The environment children grow up in will determine their long term behaviour. How they see you act and behave will become their actions and behaviour.

Master Yip recited the first Ovi dynasty moral;

"I have heard many stories about parents who have hurt their children so much, planting many seeds of suffering in them. But I believe that the parents did not mean to plant those seeds. They did not intend to make their children suffer. Maybe they received the same kind of seeds from their parents. There is a continuation in

the transmission of seeds and their father and mother might have gotten those seeds from their grandfather and grandmother. Most of us are *victims* of a kind of living that is not mindful, and the practice of mindful living, of meditation, can stop these kinds of suffering and end the transmission of such sorrow to our children and grandchildren. We can break the cycle by not allowing these kinds of seeds of suffering to be transmitted to our children, our friends, or anyone else."

"Planting seeds of suffering. That is such a powerful thing to say." Said Master Yip. "What is the wisdom you can take from that?"

I had an idea of what I wanted to say however, I didn't know how to say it. Master Yip added;

"We can break the cycle by not allowing these kinds of **seeds** of **suffering** to be transmitted to our children, our friends, or anyone else."

I blurted out a random sound, the first thing I could think of. "How we talk to our kids affects them!"

"Half right." Came the response. "Think different" Master Yip added.

"How we talk to children and.......err .... how we treat them."

"Well done Ovi. Exactly right. What we say and how we treat them will have a detrimental effect on their life, they take on the beliefs that their parents have and the opinions their parents have. I could go on and on and on..."

Tommy and Jasmine sat transfixed hanging on every word.

"I remember reading Philip Larkin's poem about parents years ago but didn't pay any attention to it." I said.

They fcku you up, your mum and dad. They may not mean to, but they do. They fill you with the faults they had and add some extra, just for you.

360 –Degree Power Thoughts

I love life. I am glad to be alive!

Tommy and Jasmine looked at each other with a guilty gaze. "What are we doing to Tommy Junior?" Said Jasmine.

"What children hear you say and see you do; they will copy. It really isn't rocket science. On the slate was an old Ovi Dynasty secret. It went something like this."

If children live with criticism,
They learn to **condemn**.
If children live with hostility,
They learn to **fight**.
If children live with ridicule,
They learn to be **shy**.
If children live with shame,
They learn to feel **guilty**.

If children live with encouragement,
They learn **confidence**.
If children live with tolerance,
They learn to be **patient**.

If children live with praise,
They learn to **appreciate**.
If children live with acceptance,
They learn to **love**.
If children live with approval,
They learn to **like themselves.**
If children live with honesty,
They learn **truthfulness**.
If children live with security,
They learn to have **faith** in themselves
and others.
If children live with friendliness,
They learn the world is a **nice** place in which to live.

"Master Yip asked me a question, I will ask you the same question now; can we stop being conditioned?" There was a long silence so I added. "Tommy, when you teach your fighting drills, what are you really doing?"

"Teaching people to fight." Came the reply.

"And what about the dance teacher, what do they do?"

"Teach people to dance"

"What is 'teaching'?"

"It's when you help someone to learn.....I think. I don't know"

"So, teaching is a form of conditioning. However, remember that we cannot teach anyone anything, they have to discover it for themselves. We as teachers, parents, brothers, sisters and friends cannot teach anyone anything. **We can only help them to discover the truth for themselves**."

Reality three on the **slave hand** is;

Learning is self discovery.

And in answer to the question, 'can we stop being conditioned' the answer is no;

A – Always

B – Being

C – Conditioned

As the days, weeks and months came and went I began to realise what a journey I was on and the journey I had been on all my life. Unfortunately I was about to find out how wrong I was. This was the hardest *reality* for me to accept and believe.

"Ovi," said Master Yip, "your life has never been a journey. No one's life is ever a journey. I know that the outside media tell of the journeys our lives take but this is not the *truth* they are conditioning you to believe that. They want to control you, dominate you and keep you in your place; they manipulate you and keep you in check."

He continued "Have you ever baked a cake Ovi?"

"Yes"

"How did you do it?"

"I followed a recipe"

"Exactly, you followed a recipe. Or to be exact a *process*." He smiled only for the second time ever. "I am going to give you the recipe or the process for life. Follow this and you will win every time.

Jasmine and Tommy sat listening with great concentration.

"Would you like to know what that recipe or process is?" I asked.

"YES"

"Then I shall show you exactly as Master Yip did with me. You will need a pen and a piece of paper. Here are the rules. The aim of the learning is to be the one to say twenty. If you say twenty you have won, if I say twenty then I am the *victor*. Rule one I must start, rule two we can only go up in multiples of one or two. It will become obvious when we start, don't worry. Tommy, Jasmine and I will play, I want you to write down the number that Jasmine says. Not mine. The numbers that Jasmine says. Clear?"

"Clear"

"I shall begin. Two"

Jasmine replied "Three"

"Write that down Tommy. Five." I added

"Six" Said Jasmine.

"Eight"

"Nine" was the reply

I came back with "Eleven"

Jasmine thought about it for a while, "Twelve."

"Fourteen" I said

"Fifteen" said Jasmine shaking her head.

"Seventeen"

"Eighteen" said Jasmine

"Twenty, I win"

"What do I do with the numbers I have written down?" Asked Tommy

"OK, what were Jasmines numbers?"

"Three, six, nine, twelve, Fifteen, and eighteen" Tommy said

"Your turn Tommy. However I will start again but you can't say any of the numbers Jasmine said, so you will need that piece of paper. Let me start two."

"So I have to say a different number to Jasmine?"

"Yes."

"Then I say four"

I came back with "Five"

"Seven" said Tommy

"Eight"

Tommy looking confused looked at the piece of paper and said "Ten"

"Eleven" I said.

"Thirteen" Added Tommy.

"Fourteen"

"Mm sixteen." said a confused Tommy

"Seventeen" was my reply.

"Nineteen"

"Twenty, I win again! How did I do it?"

"You started." Said Tommy

"That's right, but most important I knew what the winning process was and I stuck to it. Like baking a cake, if you change the recipe you will get a different result. All I had to do was be the first to start and stick to the winning formula. Two, five, eight, eleven, fourteen, seventeen and twenty."

The Ovi dynasty's fourth *reality was that life is a process, not a journey.*

360 –Degree Power Thoughts

I am willing to take action every day. I am reaching my destiny.

The final *reality in the slave hand* is one of the modern day success killers; it has become a fatal social disease. Indeed, it has the ability to totally take away your capacity to become successful.

The Ovi dynasty called it "*The OP Effect*" Worldwide the population of every country is spreading this. It is passed on from generation to generation; unfortunately people don't know that they are a carrier. It really is like a virus.

The OP Effect is "Auto-Pilot" or "*Auto-Pilot syndrome*"

Billions of people come home from work and do the same things at the same time. It's a habit, a repetitive, dull existence. One that keeps us from growing and achieving the extraordinary. "Do you know what I mean by extraordinary?" I asked Tommy and Jasmine.

Before either answered I rudely continued. "Sorry, but Tommy you said you wouldn't mind a bit of memory loss for my wealth. What do you do to *invite* into your life, to achieve the wealth you want?"

"I'm not with you" Tommy said

"To be different. You know; special, remarkable, exceptional or odd. Odd is good by the way. To be any of those things you need to be willing to do something no one else is willing to do. Listen carefully, everyone you meet would love to be rich or wealthy; the issue is they are unwilling to break their routine or their way of life.................their Auto-pilot."

Master Yip was exceptional at explaining **Auto-Pilot syndrome.**

"Ovi," said Master Yip. "Do you have friends?"

"Yes, but not many. Why?"

"I don't know your friends but I can tell you what they do. Are you ready?"

"Not really but........" That was my non conformist side showing. "Sorry but I'm confused."

"Pay attention." Master Yip said "The Ovi Dynasty realised that we are a nation, no not a nation but a world of snowflakes. A snowflake is an individual who will do the absolute minimum to survive. Working 9 to 5 means that they get up at 7.30am, shower and get to work five minutes before its time to start. They finish work come home, watch TV, browse social media (for hours to spy on people they don't like, or know) then bed to sleep. A snowflake is a loser. But they don't know it."

Master Yip continued "I'm sorry to say that you have become a snowflake Ovi. You do what others anticipate you will do. You do your best. Your best. Unfortunately your best is way below what is needed to win or achieve anything of note. YOUR BEST IS NOT GOOD ENOUGH. Please do not do your best. Do what is necessary. Listen to my words. DO WHAT IS NECESSARY. Not your best, your best will never be good enough."

Master Yip took the white sheet from the second slate wall. He drew a circle and said "This is the *Auto-Pilot* button; every button is set to default. It is set to the ON position. You are born with it set to the on position, you go through life never knowing there are any other settings."

He then drew four lines that came out of the circle; they pointed North, South, East and West.

He then began to fill in the missing information.

Steals behaviour from the past.

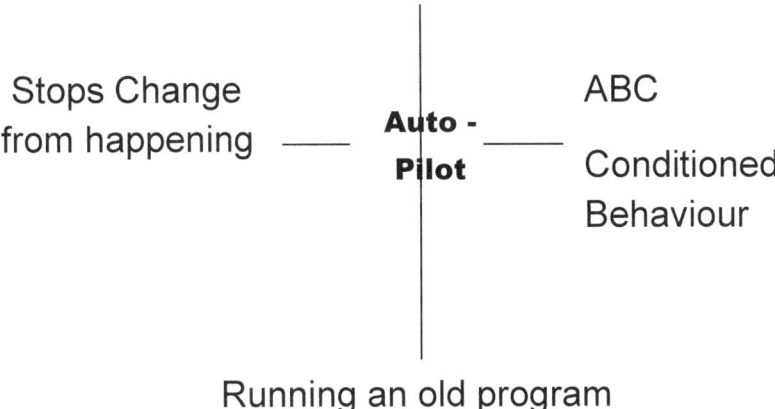

Stops Change from happening — **Auto - Pilot** — ABC Conditioned Behaviour

Running an old program

"As you can see Ovi, a mind on Auto-Pilot will never have the capacity to achieve anything beyond what they have already accomplished. It's time for your meditation. Tomorrow will be a testing day for you."

The following day would prove to be a turning point in my decision to stay. You see of the seven hands; **hand five** would prove to be the backbone of the seven. I was about to get my first taste of **hand five** but really didn't realise it at the time.

On the slate wall Master Yip had written down the **five realities of the slave hand.**

Hand 1- The Slave

Slave to our habits

The ABC of behaviour

Learning is about self discovery

Life is a process not a journey

The OP effect

"So, what now?" said Master Yip. He continued "What use are they to you?"

"I now know what has stopped me from success in the past"

"What use is that to you?"

"I know where I have gone wrong in the past?"

"What use is that to you?"

Here we go again, is that all Master Yip can say.

"Ovi, look at the **five realities** what use are they to you?"

"I now understand what I need to do to succeed"

"Ovi, look at the **five realities** what use are they to you? Is an understanding enough? Let me put it another way. You need to dig a hole and you have a shovel, is knowing how to use the shovel enough to dig the hole?"

"No."

"Ovi success is a science. It does not happen by chance. Just like life itself you have to have the correct conditions for the result you want."

Master Yip continued

"When the winds of change blow, some people build walls and others build windmills. It's our resistance to what is that will create more suffering."

Standing, Master Yip said "Meditation time Ovi. Tomorrow you will learn the **hand five**"

It's not who you are underneath…it's what you do that defines you.

It's not who you are underneath...it's what you do that defines you.

It's not who you are underneath...it's what you do that defines you.

360 –Degree Power Thoughts

I forgive myself and set myself free.

Chapter 4

Hand Five

An enigma within an enigma

If you plan for one year, plant rice. If you plan for ten years, plant trees. If you plan for 100 years, educate mankind.

Tommy and Jasmine were totally transfixed with my words, sat waiting for the next instalment.

"It's important you fully understand what happened to me out there." I said. "Let me tell you about the place I called home for 12 years. I was confused as to how I got there; sure, I remember the plane falling from the sky. I remember clinging to the debris; but I also remember the ride in the truck to the monastery, but according to Master Yip they found me at the gates of the abbey, bleeding and bruised. Who was right?"

I told Tommy and Jasmine about the conversation Master Yip and I had as we walked the grounds. I had been there around 18 months and at this point all I had learnt was;

The truth is the only law that matters

I still didn't know what that was about. Listen, I was a young man from a working class background from a small mining village. I was a nobody, a nothing; not even in employment. Divorced, bankrupt and living above a shop on the high street.

Meditation after meditation did not bring the answer. Bring an empty cup? I felt like I was on an episode of survivor; just waiting for the TV crew to turn up and say surprise! What two words? Oh and the *truth;* that was beginning to really get to me. 18 months in and all Master Yip had told me the *first hand – the slave hand.*

Sitting with Tommy and Jasmine I knew exactly why it had taken eighteen months to get this far. I had not mastered *hand five*. Master Yip was well aware of this, so in his infinite wisdom he decided to enlighten me. In my defence, he nor anyone in the learning space had not introduced that concept. Well, I do remember a conversation about a spade and digging a hole. I think that may have been a clue.

"Ovi, do you know why I gave you that name?" Master Yip asked as we walked past the abbey.

"I had wondered, it is clearly related to the Ovi dynasty. I don't know why you think I have anything in common with the world's greatest empire?"

"Survival. I feel a storm coming." Said Master Yip.

"Then let's head back to the monastery."

"No Ovi, a storm in you. A storm in a storm. You are the storm and what is raging inside you right now is an ever greater storm" He continued "Remember our conversation*............... Ovi success is a science. It does not happen by chance. Just like life itself you have to have the correct conditions for the result you want.*"

"Yes, yes I do"

"Ovi there is no such thing as coincidence, chance or accident. You make your own luck and fate is something you control. I see something in you that no other living human being has ever shown to me. *Survival*."

It's true I was a born survivor. The things I had gone through in the past would have finished most people off. The cancer nearly did, I fought back and took control. The divorce, the money issues and of course losing family members so close together. I dug deep, really deep.

"Ovi, we did not bring you here. You made it over 50 miles from the crash site to the entrance of the abbey. Survival instinct? I don't know, but it got you here."

"I've got it. Attraction, it's meant to be. I attracted it."

"Ovi there is no such thing. There is only one law in the entire world and it is not attraction. That is fiction, creative writing and illusion. It keeps the rich rich and the poor poor."

"Then what.................."

"Stop! Have you learnt nothing? The only law that matters is the law of **truth**, you know that."

"Yes but I don't know what that is, no one does!"

"Self discovery Ovi. You will discover the **truth** in your own time. No one can tell you or show you. You must discover it when you are ready. The Ovi dynasty survived for over 900 years, they were global leaders in mining, building, innovation and many other industries. No other company came close to their dominance. The **seven hands** made that a guarantee, the **encoded master messages** were a stroke of genius, who would have thought something so simple could change the world. Well your world?"

Finally Master Yip said "The **truth** Ovi is that you did make it here without any help from anyone. **Your truth** may be different."

It's not who you are underneath...it's what you do that defines you.

360 –Degree Power Thoughts

Life begins at the edge of your comfort zone.

I decided it was time to take a break; it was around midnight in early December so it was cold, but that didn't stop us sitting out on the patio with a warm drink.

"Tommy you clearly have read lots of self help books?" I said as the cold breath faded into the light.

"Yes, everything from Carnegie to Gladwell, why do you ask?"

"OK" I continued "How has your life changed as a result of reading those books?"

Tommy thought for a while; then said "I feel better about myself"

"OK, that's fine but how has your life changed?"

After a short silence Tommy said "It hasn't."

"Tommy" I asked "What do the books say about PMA?"

"That's easy Positive Mental Attitude!" Tommy replied with sense of pride.

"Tommy; Tommy; Tommy you have fallen victim to *hand one; the slave* ABC Always Being Conditioned. The self development revolution of the

70's and 80's conditioned us to believe it meant Positive Mental Attitude. They; the few; the people in the know want to make you feel better about yourself, but they don't want you to have what they have. They want to keep you coming back for a boost of positivity."

"PMA stands for something very different and it's the difference between success and failure."

Master Yip explained to me the first **truth** to **hand five**.

He started by asking me a question. "Ovi, why do self improvement programs fail?"

"I don't know"

"Let me put it a different way. You have an individual who is highly educated with degrees awash. She has great ideas and concepts whizzing around her head, but she is stuck in a job she hates and has been so for the past 10 years. Then you have the college dropout. He decided to quit his education to pursue his dream. Now he owns a successful business. What was the difference between the two?"

That was a rhetorical question I was to later find out as I tried to answer Master Yip's enigma.

"Ovi, the five realities will help you to understand why self improvement programs and books fail."

Reality one;

We Fear Change

Face this fact; no matter what type of self-improvement strategy you are using, at some point you are going to have to make a CHANGE.
It could be a small change, or a big change, but you are going to have to get out of your "comfort zone". Our subconscious "conditioned mind" does not like change. In fact, it is designed to resist change and to keep us where we are. The reason for this is the subconscious is primarily a survival mechanism. Its primary function is survival. It perceives any type of change as a threat to our survival. Unless we can bypass our survival mechanism (SUPER SUBCONSCIOUS), all of our self-improvement attempts will fail.

"The Ovi dynasty thrived on change" said Master Yip. "They knew that was the only constant the world had. When the motor car was invented the people hated it at first. Yes they wanted to get from A to B in the fastest time possible; but if you asked them how to do that they said 'a faster horse'. Two things to consider here Ovi; one is the fact that we

89

are conditioned to fear change and two; we are born with an inbuilt safety feature that stops us taking risks, we see them as a hazard or a point of danger."

I looked at Tommy and Jasmine and asked them to write down the only 3 guarantees in life.

"I can only think of one" Said Jasmine. "Death; at some point everyone will die."

"Well done, any idea of the other two?"

"No."

"The second is that everyone will pay TAX at some point in their life. You buy a bus ticket; you pay tax; you buy chocolate or chicken; you will pay tax."

"And the third?" asked Jasmine.

"Change! Everything changes; the seasons change. Try stopping that!"

I continued;

"Look at the first Model T Ford all those years back; now look at the advance in technology; massive change. I could go on and on and give example after example. Think about your life and how it has changed. Every aspect of your existence is constantly changing. We now have a device that fits into the palm of our hand that can play music; we can talk to anyone in the world with the push of a couple of buttons; we can even play videos."

I smiled. "When I left for India the mobile phone had just been introduced; it was the size of a brick and needed a battery the size of a small suitcase to power it. We live in changing times; we always have."

Master Yip told me he would show me how to embrace change. He said that when I discover the **truth** change would become part of me.

360 –Degree Power Thoughts

Life created me to be successful.

Reality two.

We Seek Instant Results

Today people are conditioned by the media advertising to expect "instant results." Hence they want it NOW and expect to see results immediately in one session, one day, one week, one chapter, etc. They give most self-improvement techniques and practices one shot, and if they do not get immediate results, they get discouraged and give up.

Immediate results are always possible, but sometimes we need time to align our energy with our desires. If we do not align our energy properly, we will not reach our goal. The need for instant results or instant gratification often keeps people from taking the time to align their energy, so it actually takes them LONGER to reach their goals.

I looked at both Tommy and Jasmine who were sat together on the patio furniture under the patio heater.

"Master Yip explained to me how and why instant results are both a good thing and a bad obsession," I said.

"Take the person who wants to diet. They do get instant results within two weeks provided they follow the plan or the process; they will begin to see the results they want. Then they become lazy and fall back into the old habits. The weight goes back on and suddenly the diet no longer works, in fact you decide that the diet is not for you and then you move on to the next; then the next; and so on."

Our quest for instant results stops us from gaining long term success.

Reality three

We are "TRYING" instead of "DOING"

Most people "try" to get what they want. The problem is every time you try, you are setting yourself up for failure. In reality you can't try to do anything. You either DO it or you DON'T. The whole world is trying and most are failing. People "try" self-improvement programs and immediately set themselves up for failure. I see it all the time. The worst ones are those who write and inquire about a refund BEFORE they even order the program!

They say something like, "I want to be sure I can get my money back if this doesn't work". This tells me that they only want to "try" it, and of course, they will fail. Then they can blame the program for their failure.

Master Yip removed the cover from the slate wall; it said;

"The successful person has the habit of doing the things failures don't like to do. They don't like doing them either necessarily. But their disliking is subordinated to the strength of their purpose."

Reality four

Doing What You Know

I'm sure you know people who have studied personal improvement materials most of their lives and have not made any SIGNIFICANT changes. They read, study and attend self-improvement seminars and nothing, or very little, seems to change.

Why is this so?

Simply because they are self-improvement "junkies". Like any junkie they need a "fix". But the problem is that even though it is a positive fix, they are still addicts. They are addicted to the illusion that the more they study and learn, the more their life will improve. If they can just find that one book, one program, one strategy they are looking for, their lives will turn around.

Of course, they never find it because they are addicted to COLLECTING INFORMATION; they don't move forward.

"Ovi," said Master Yip "The last *reality* in this hand is the key to the other four. Indeed it is the crucial source of all lasting success. **Without this the empire that the Ovi dynasty built would not have even have made it past the first day!"**

Master Yip told me that he would tell me the final *reality* after 30 days.

"What do I do for 30 days?" I questioned.

"What do you do? Meditate of course!"

I looked at Tommy and Jasmine, two hard working people with a new baby; Tommy Junior was just six weeks old and by the sound of the racket coming from upstairs it was feeding time.

"Let's take a break, Tommy Junior needs you."

Tommy was a hands-on dad and it was his turn to feed Junior; so Jasmine and I chatted in the lounge.

"So how did you make your money, I mean OviTec, what did it do?" Asked Jasmine

"To be honest I have signed a confidentiality clause that stops me telling anyone what we did. Let's just say I invented something that the defence industry really wanted, and were willing to pay a premium for. And to be honest, that's nothing compared to what's to come!"

Tommy came back down eager to continue our story. "Where were we?" he questioned as he sat down in the chair next to the baby monitor.

360 –Degree Power Thoughts

I am in the process of positive change.

"The last *reality* of this hand." I said as I sat under the lamp in the corner of the room.

"My 30 days of meditation came to an end and I felt different, changed; dare I say it transformed." I told Tommy and Jasmine. "I was intrigued to find out what the last *reality* in this hand was. Oh, and Tommy, this is where you find out what to do with books you have read."

"Why do you think I have brought you here Ovi?" Master Yip softly said.

"The Library?" I said. The door to this room has been locked since I arrived here. A vast expanse of knowledge locked up; why?

"Ovi, what use are these books?"

"They give you knowledge," I replied.

"Yes Ovi, that is correct. Is having knowledge enough to succeed in life?"

"You need it to achieve anything," I continued "knowledge is essential to success; without it you don't know what to do."

Master Yip repeated "Ovi, what use are these books?"

"Is this about the shovel?" I asked "You know digging a hole."

"Yes Ovi it is; I believe you are ready to tell me the use of a shovel and a library full of books; tell me Ovi have you discovered it for yourself?"

"I have..."

Tommy and Jasmine were sat waiting for me to give them the answer; they were in for a surprise, I sat in silence.

Looking out of the window I was both surprised and taken aback when I saw the snow falling from the shadowy clouds.

As we stood on the patio watching the indistinguishable white flakes of frozen water descend from the gloomy ibis, Tommy suddenly noticed that the shed door was open and the snow was covering the lawn mower.

"I need to close the shed door." Tommy began to walk towards the shed; I grabbed his arm and stopped him.

"Tommy is knowing the door needs to be closed enough?"

"What; all I know is if I don't close the door I will need a new mower."

"So; is knowing what to do enough to save the mower?"

"No I need to close the door!" I let go of Tommy's arm; he closed the door and locked it. "Wait!" shouted Tommy "now I know what to do with the books."

"And that is...what exactly?" Jasmine asked.

"I need to take action. I need to act on what I know."

"Tommy you need PMA. *Positive Massive Action*."

"Sometimes the hardest part isn't letting go but rather learning to start over."

Master Yip's words resonated with me, it echoed like a wish in a well, you know like when throw you money in and make a wish, and all day long you look for signs that your desire has been granted.

"Ovi," said Master Yip "Nothing else matters. Listen very carefully Ovi; you have learnt so much in your stay here and now is the time to learn the most important lesson that the Ovi dynasty discovered. For every learning point or lesson learnt the Ovi dynasty would take two positive actions. They would never look to learn anything else until they had put into practice what they had already learnt."

PMA;

Positive Massive Action. Take two positive steps on what you have learnt.

"Ovi. Knowledge is not power! You have been conditioned to believe that knowledge is power. It is only potential power. You have to use the knowledge for the power to be released. PMA Positive Massive Action"

The Ovi dynasty had an ancient rule that took them to global dominance for 900 years and it was this;

Take Positive Massive Action. If you want to break your cycle of failure, disappointment and frustration then **you** must also take action on your new found knowledge.

"Tommy, I want you and Jasmine to make a commitment right now; when you discover the **truth**; use it. Use it make your life better; tell Junior how to use it. I want you to take two positive steps right now; knowing what you know now, what will you change with immediate effect? I want you to write it down and keep it with you at all times. Do it now, write it down."

Now it is your turn. Write down two positive actions you will do with immediate effect.

1.

2.

360 –Degree Power Thoughts

I rise above my own self imposed limitations.

Chapter 5

Hand Two

Respect for the 5

Three years had now passed and Master Yip told me I was ready for the next hand. Likewise, I told Tommy and Jasmine to work on and take Positive Massive Action on what we had discovered. It wasn't fair keeping them up all night. Tommy junior needed their undivided attention. We made arrangements for me to come back same time next week.

Tommy and Jasmine thought that I was helping them to become successful; in reality they were helping me. I needed to tell someone; Master Yip insisted I teach the *truth*.

There I was back with Tommy and Jasmine, this time I brought food; thought I would return the favour.

"Things haven't always been so peaceful" Master Yip told me as we sat beneath the *truth* statue; a five thousand year old sculpture forged from gold. I suppose a lasting effigy of the wealth that the Ovi dynasty had amassed. "Before the Ovi empire had discovered the *truth* and taught it to the many there was fighting, unrest and struggle."

Master Yip stood and said "Look Ovi, what do you see?"

I looked at the sprawling hills and beautiful countryside that surrounded us for miles. "I see stillness and tranquillity."

"The land you see before you were battle grounds; bloody clashes from rival tribes and gangs. Conflict was rife and thousands of men, women and children lost their life. Ovi, the *truth* ended the bloody battles and brought the warring factions together. The Ovi dynasty had found the one thing that would bring peace and harmony to this land. The hard part was not in its discovery but in its acceptance."

"How so..?"

"Ovi, the *truth* is within you right now; it always has been, as it was for the soldiers that fought here; as it is with all living creatures. Just because you have it does not mean you want to believe or acknowledge its existence. Remember this Ovi; we cannot teach, only help people to discover the *truth*."

Master Yip turned and said "follow me."

We walked to the learning space;

I paid my respects to the scrolls and sat, I waited for my next lesson.

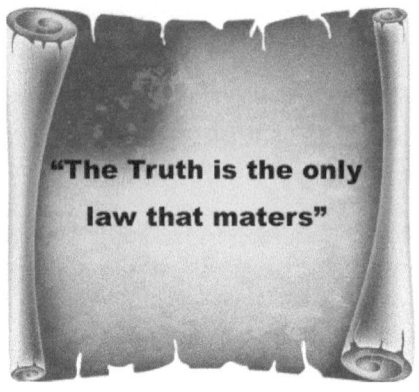

"The Truth is the only law that maters"

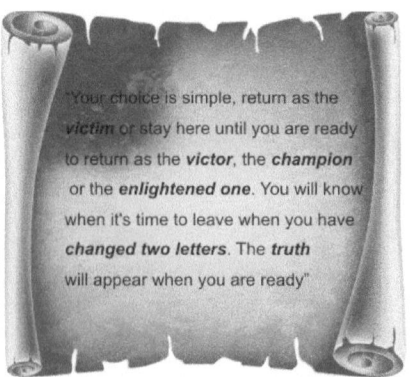

"Your choice is simple, return as the victim or stay here until you are ready to return as the victor, the champion or the enlightened one. You will know when it's time to leave when you have changed two letters. The truth will appear when you are ready"

"Let me take you back to hand one; the **slave hand**.

I have added a little detail to this;

98% of the world's population will not act on the **truth** learning; only 2% will feel the freedom and embrace their new life." Continuing Master Yip added.

"Ovi, our habits are a powerful force that takes a little time to break free from. You must learn new; more empowering habits. One last question for today Ovi; to be part of that 2% who will find the **truth** you will have to beat your competition; tell me, who is your competition Ovi?"

Reality One

10 Words

Master Yip left me all alone in the learning space, as he disappeared down the long corridor he said; "you will find the answer down by the water."

I spent the best part of the day looking but did not find anything. Heading back to find Master Yip, as the sun was setting, I found him in the great hall.

"Tell me Ovi; what did you find?"

"I looked everywhere but couldn't find anything. There was nothing new there."

"I know. The thing you are looking for has been there all the time."

"Well," I added "I did my best."

"Ovi, you are falling into your old habits. Your best is not good enough. Do what is necessary; not your best. Go back to the water and return only when you have done what is necessary."

It was obvious that Tommy and Jasmine didn't follow what I was talking about. I had brought some items with me to show them; it was important that they discover this for themselves.

I handed them a small compact mirror, the kind you get in a makeup department shop. "The answer you are looking for is inside there" I said.

"The biggest fight of your life is with the person you are looking at. I realised that, as I sat looking into the calm water in the monastery; I saw myself looking back. As I sat gazing at my reflection an overwhelming feeling of ownership hit me. I mean in that second I realised that I and I alone had brought me to this point in my life. It wasn't the divorce; it was my reaction to it. It wasn't losing family members; it was how I reacted to it."

"Ovi, I am going to give you ten words that will change your life. Ten simple words that if you are able to accept into your daily life and will revolutionise the results you get."

Master Yip was holding a small piece of white cloth that was folded over a number of times. He began to unfold the delicate material to reveal a small round coin like object.

"Take this Ovi; keep it with you at all times as a reminder of your old habits and actions. More importantly, it will serve as a master for your future"

Master Yip then placed the pendant in my hand; "it is yours to keep on one condition; you will follow the **truth plan**."

"**Truth plan,** what is that?"

"You will learn...in time; here keep this safe Ovi."

If it is to be

it is up to me

(10 life changing words)

360 –Degree Power Thoughts

Humour and fun contribute to my well being.

"Ovi. You and you only have the power to become an unstoppable energy; a power of strength not only for you but for everyone you meet. You must make the **truth** available for everyone. There is too much traffic in people's heads. Ovi help them to take control; don't worry this will all make sense when you are ready."

"Just like the Egyptians; the Ovi dynasty elders and founders built secret tombs and rooms underground." Master Yip said these rooms were never meant to be found. Just like the Egyptians, they buried their most valuable possessions where no one would think of looking. Unlike the Egyptians, the Ovi dynasty did not collect diamonds and jewels. Their most valuable possession was the **truth**. "Ovi in one tomb we found their most valuable artefacts."

Master Yip presented me with two thin grey slates with an inscription on each one. The first said;

The past is the present, isn't it? It's the future too.

The second said;

There is no present or future, only the past, happening over and over again, right now.

Reality Two

Perception

I delved into the bag I had brought with me to Tommy and Jasmine's; "here; look at the words on this piece paper. What do they say?"

"That's easy" Jasmine said, "Good times are here, what do think Tommy?"

"Well, yes I agree; but good times are here?" He questioned.

"Listen if there is one thing I can say with 100% certainty and confidence it's this. How you view the world is in direct alignment with the past conditioning you have had; A B C. It also dictates your future behaviour."

"Do you know how to train a monkey?" I asked.

"No"

"Then let me enlighten you.......................

Start with a cage containing five monkeys.

Inside the cage, hang a banana on a string and place a set of stairs under it. Before long, a monkey will go to the stairs and start to climb towards the banana.

As soon as he touches the stairs, spray *all* of the monkeys with cold water. After a while, another monkey makes an attempt with the same result - *all* the monkeys are sprayed with cold water.

Pretty soon, when another monkey tries to climb the stairs, the other monkeys will try to prevent it.

Now, turn off the cold water.

Remove one monkey from the cage and replace it with a new one. The new monkey sees the banana and wants to climb the stairs. To his surprise and horror, all of the other monkeys attack him.

After another attempt and attack, he knows that if he tries to climb the stairs, he will be assaulted. Next, remove another of the original five monkeys and replace it with a new one.

The newcomer goes to the stairs and is attacked. The previous newcomer takes part in the punishment with enthusiasm. Again, replace a third original monkey with a new one. The new one makes it to the stairs and is attacked as well. Two of the four monkeys that beat him have no idea why they were not permitted to climb the stairs, or why they are participating in the beating of the newest monkey.

After replacing the fourth and fifth original monkeys, all the monkeys that have been sprayed with cold water have been replaced. Nevertheless, no monkey ever again approaches the stairs. Let me make one thing very clear. That's cruel and not something I condone. It does however prove that our past conditioning has a huge factor in our present and future behaviour."

I handed out a second piece of paper with the same letters on as the first; but this time I had removed the box that obscured the bottom part of the letters

The look of surprise and shock on their faces was a picture. "Hold them up together" I instructed.

Perception. What the eyes see and the ears hear; the mind believes.

Human beings do not act in this world according to what is real. They act according to their perceptions of reality.

Reality Three

If you want your outer world to change you must first change your inner world

"Ovi, first you must understand that your outer world; your possessions, the things you own are a direct reflection of your state of mind."

Sitting next to me Master Yip was aware of my history back in the UK; I had told him about my troubles.

"Ovi; I know this is something you will find hard to both believe and have faith in; you must understand that this is the start of you discovering the *truth*. People; both good and bad have thoughts racing around in their head. Think about this, the person with debt and worry in their life will plant tiny seeds or thoughts in their head about the debt and worry. We grow crops here Ovi; we take PMA to ensure that the crop in our fields are the crop we want. How do we do that?!

"Exactly as you said, you take Positive Massive Action."

"So, if we didn't plant the seeds we know will bring us the crop we want; what will happen?"

"If you didn't purposefully plant seed then weeds will grow."

"Ovi, weeds will automatically grow. Do you know why?"

"No."

"They will automatically grow because someone else has planted them. Just like the birds when they drop seed from the sky; they don't mean to, it's just a part of nature. If we didn't work the land every day then weeds will appear; we work in the fields to prevent the weeds taking over; despite the fact we plant the correct crop each year we will still have to contend with the weeds. We work hard to both plant fresh seeds and banish the wild unwanted weeds."

As I spoke to Tommy and Jasmine about Master Yip's explanation; I could sense questions were on their way.

"AJ I'm not sure that I know where this is leading" Said Tommy.

"It's easy, your brain is the fertile field ready for either crops or wild weeds; what grows there is entirely your choice and your decision. Master Yip then asked me a question...."

"Ovi, when you were back in England did you socialise with friends?"

My answer was "yes, we would have drinks on a Thursday and Sunday together."

Master Yip continued, "When you get back to the UK; what do you think your friends will be doing?"

"I don't know." I replied.

"I do," Master Yip added, "they will be doing exactly the same thing. The same thing they and you were doing before you decided to get out."

Master yip wrote on the slate wall

100 people

"Ovi, in general people work for around 40 to 45 years in their lifetime. During that time they have the chance to build a life and prepare for retirement.

At the age of 65, having worked for 45 years here is what will have happened to the 100."

Master Yip wrote on the slate again.

5 out of 100   Dead

"like your father Ovi; dead before his time."

36 out of 100   Still working

Some are working because they **want** to; others because they **have** to.

4 out of100   OK

That means four people are 'comfortable'; living in a house they own and can afford to have a couple of holidays a year and have limited disposable income.

54 out of 100 broke, flat broke.

Living from day to day; repeating yesterday today and tomorrow.

1 out of 100   Wealthy

Financially independent with a strong net worth.

360 –Degree Power Thoughts

I am always able to make the correct decision I recognise my own ability.

"Let me ask you another question Ovi," Master Yip said. "If you wanted to become a doctor where would you go? What would you do?"

"I would go to medical school? Where is this leading?"

"Listen and learn. Out of the 100; If you want to be OK; you know 'comfortable'; living in a house you own and can afford to have a couple of holidays a year and have limited disposable income, who would you ask?"

"Is this a trick question? I would find and ask the four people who were in that bracket and ask them what they have done to achieve it." I answered.

"Well done, and no it is not a trick question." Master Yip continued "If you wanted to be part of the elite, the 1%; the wealthy, who would you ask for advice?"

"I would find and ask the one who had made that happen, are you sure this is not a trick question?"

"No tricks Ovi, just one last observation; Why, why, why did you spend your time associating with the 54? You ask the very people for advice that are not qualified to answer your question. You ask your friends what, how, when and why. How do I make more money? How do I get out of the debt I am in? The people you are asking are the same as you. If they knew how to answer that question; they wouldn't be in the 54 bracket."

I turned to Tommy and Jasmine and said. "When I got back to England and things had died down a little, I went back on Thursday and Sunday to the same bar I frequented all those years ago. Tell me Tommy; what did I find?"

Shaking his head he said "I don't know."

"I do," added Jasmine. "The same people repeating the same behaviour that they did 20 years ago."

"And there you have it." I said "Jasmine that was a stroke of genius."

Master Yip reminded me of a previous learning; "*Ovi, success and failure are a science. You have to have the right conditions for what you want to achieve. Remember life is a process; not a journey.*"

He continued "The laws or rules of farming are identical to the laws and rules of inner success. (**If you want your outer world to change you must first change your inner world**). If you want to harvest the seeds you plant in your inner world you must make sure that they are the right seeds."

"Think of your mind as a jigsaw puzzle" said Master Yip. "When you are born that jigsaw puzzle is blank, untouched and pure."

In time that blank jigsaw will pull towards you
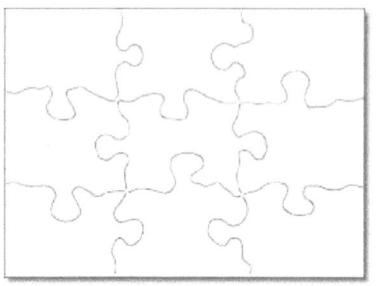
pieces to fit in with what you have been taught or conditioned to believe. That jigsaw then becomes your default behaviour; Your ***Auto-Pilot or Your Truth***

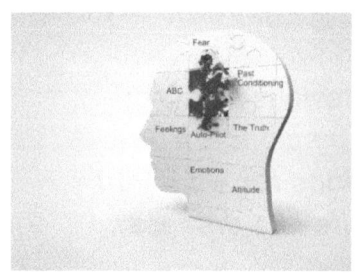
This would prove to be one of my most difficult times at the monastery for me. Master Yip was about to tell me what seeds and weeds had to do with my future success and past failure.

"What is a seed Ovi?"

"Something you plant." I replied.

"Correct. Something you plant. Then what happens to it?"

After some thought; I said "It grows."

"Yes, it grows. So we have to plant the seeds we want; to produce the crop or result we want. We also have to make sure that we take out the weeds that will automatically grow. The weeds planted by others and ourselves. The Ovi dynasty found out that planting seeds in the ground was identical to planting seeds in the mind. Some seeds were crops and had a positive effect on our behaviour; and others were weeds; they had a very negative, unhelpful and harmful effect on our behaviour and ultimately kill our success."

Master Yip continued, "listen very carefully Ovi; from the age of zero to six many seeds and weeds have been planted in our vulnerable brains. Fears and phobias that our parents had are now ours. Their behaviour is now our behaviour."

"I understand what a seed is, the kind you plant in the ground, I also know how to plant it. What I don't understand is what seeds get planted in our head and how do they get there?" I asked.

"Ovi, conditioning is the key and happens in many ways. One way we can be conditioned is by language. What and how we say things to others and more importantly what and how we say things to ourselves. This is the starting point to changing past negative behaviour. The Ovi dynasty calls this **upholding.** Some people call it self-talk others affirmations; but the Ovi dynasty traced it back to its roots. **Upholding;** it means preservation or protection. Protection of your right to be wealthy. And as for what it is and how it gets there; let me take you back to the beginning."

Before I continued telling Tommy and Jasmine about the **Upholding** I had to make sure that they fully understood about self-talk and affirmations.

"Can I ask you both? Do you know what an affirmation is?"

Jasmine was quick to answer. "Yes, it's when you talk to yourself."

"Correct! Tell me more" I said

"Its self-talk, you know the words in your head."

"Yes, now think about the field that the farmer tends. If the farmer plants a weed what will grow?"

"I know this one" Tommy said as he stood up to look out of the window; "weeds."

"Yes. So with that in mind if you plant a negative seed or word into your head what will grow?"

Both Tommy and Jasmine were stuck for the answer; not because they didn't know it, but because they didn't know how to put it into words.

"We plant more than 70,000 seeds (words and thoughts) in our head every day; that is a combination of internal thoughts and the actual words we say. Let me ask you both; how many times have you said out loud (You Idiot?)"

"I do it all the time," said Jasmine

"Me too," added Tommy

"That is a self planted negative seed! Weeds are guaranteed to grow. And you know what happens to a negative seed or thought don't you? It turns into negative behaviour!"

"You said self planted," Jasmine questioned.

"I did and well spotted. Self planted means *you* put it there. You made it personal to you. The other of course is planted by someone else. Let me break this down in a very simple way;"

I continued to explain.

"When we plant a seed in our brain it is called language."

Seeds = Language

"Now a seed can be planted by you (self-talk or affirmation) or it can be planted by someone else; anyone. That is called conditioning. ABC"

Weeds = Language

"Now a weed can be planted by you (self-talk or affirmation) or it can be planted by someone else; anyone. That is called conditioning. ABC"

Looking at both Tommy and Jasmine I asked, "What's the difference?"

"I'm guessing one is positive and one is negative?" questioned Jasmine.

"Correct. Do you both remember the *slave hand*?"

Both Tommy and Jasmine nodded.

"*Reality five is Auto-Pilot-The OP effect*. This is so important; it is the very core of why we do what we do. I'll let Master Yip tell you."

"The Ovi dynasty discovered something that changed the whole behaviour landscape. They uncovered **a truth**; but not **THE** truth. That if both understood and acted on (Positive Massive Action) will guarantee you will be in the 1% bracket. Let me add one thing Ovi; not only do you have to understand and act on it, you must 100% believe that this is the *major truth*. Listen Ovi, there is something hidden deep within each and every one of us it's called a *self-image.* The Ovi Empire made the connection between the *self-image* and The *OP effect*."

Master Yip ended our session that day with a statement. "The *self-image* and The *OP effect* are one and the same."

Master Yip Continued. "Your auto-pilot and self-image are the same, as it is with everyone in the world. I need to draw this for you Ovi."

The Gate Keeper

The Now Mind

"Ovi this is sometimes called the conscious mind. The *dynasty* called it the Now Mind because it deals with the here and now. It decides what to keep and what to give to the Holding Mind. It is in fact a *gate keeper.*

It is designed to keep only what it needs for the now moment, like walking in and out of rooms, it stops you from bumping into things; it also keeps you aware of your surroundings to keep you safe. If the gate keeper doesn't need it; it automatically lets it go. The reference point or situation to letting it go is your past conditioning forcing you to (automatically) decide if you need it or not."

The gatekeeper works exceptionally hard; it receives millions of pieces of information each second and then runs that information through the world's most sophisticated filter. The Ovi dynasty found that the filter in modern day society is faulty; it had been hacked."

I turned to Tommy and Jasmine and said "Think of it as your PC, if the antivirus isn't working bad things begin to happen. It starts to misbehave."

Master Yip added, "Instead of keeping the unwanted stuff out it keeps it in the memory – the **Holding Mind**. It drops it into the ***conditioned-auto-pilot-self-image***. And that Ovi, is where the magic begins."

The Holding Mind stores information, with millions of pieces of unwanted information, they need to go somewhere. And with our filters broken they end up here. Every single item you think or has happened to you is here, no matter how big or how small, The Holding Mind will store it. Within

The Holding Mind you possess something called "**Picture of Reality**".

"This is *your* Picture of Reality. Ovi let me tell you an old *Empire* saying. **The only reality is the one you see**. Can you tell me what that means?"

"Honestly Master Yip, no."

"What is your reality now Ovi?"

"My reality is this place; it has been for five years," I replied.

"Correct; is it the only reality?"

"Yes. It's my only reality."

"I didn't ask that question Ovi," came the reply. "I asked is it *the* only reality?"

"At the moment it is," I answered.

"For the first time ever Ovi, I may have to teach you instead of you discovering. One last question; is this reality here the same as the reality in England?"

"No; they are totally different, why?"

"I'll answer your question with a question. Was that your only reality?"

I finally understood realities! **The only reality is the one you see** despite there being a reality for every single person, no every single living entity. So there are endless truths but the only reality we have is the one we see and experience on a daily basis.

"Ovi, let me tell you about the *self image* first; and then I will tell you why it is also called the *auto-pilot*. Self-image is how you see yourself in relation to others. This may be how you see yourself physically or it may be more about the idea you have of yourself, which could also be called self-concept. It is very important as it affects your self-esteem and confidence."

Master Yip had written on the slate wall the following;

Self-image includes:

- What you think you look like physically
- How your personality comes across
- What kind of person you think you are
- What you think others think of you
- How much you like yourself or you think others like you

360 –Degree Power Thoughts

Old maps do not help new journeys.

"Ovi; if you have poor self-opinion your self-esteem will be poor. How exactly are they different? Self-esteem focuses on how you feel about yourself. Image is about how you see yourself. They are, as you can see, quite close. You may believe how you see yourself is how others see you. This cannot be true. Your view of yourself is shaped by your unique thoughts and beliefs and you will have a **distorted** view. You will see yourself in a positive or negative way and both will be biased and influenced by your past conditioning. You may have a negative view of yourself and if so you are probably highly critical of yourself."

At this point Master Yip's attitude changed. He became more intense and passionate. "This will lead you to the **truth** Ovi. Listen to my words very carefully......

"If we tell ourselves over and over again that we cannot remember names then we begin to act like a person who cannot remember names. I know people who tell me that they can never remember names, maybe you know someone like that? Or when you ask someone to tell a joke they say things like "I can never remember jokes." "I'm clumsy or unlucky." "I can't lose weight." If you tell yourself something for long enough it will become a reality for you. All of a sudden we start to act like the person we come to know on the inside."

Master Yip turned to me and for the first time since I had been in the monastery he put his hands on my shoulders and said; "Ovi, it's time you took a great leap towards the *truth*. What I am about to tell you will change your world. *The way you behave; in other words the way you act or the way you conduct yourself is a direct result of your conditioned-auto-pilot-self-image. Ovi, we will always act in a manner consistent with our self image; that's why it is also your auto pilot."*

Master Yip repeated the last part of the sentence over and over again.

Ovi, we will always act in a manner consistent with our self image; that's why it is also your auto pilot."

Ovi, we will always act in a manner consistent with our self image; that's why it is also your auto pilot."

WE WILL ALWAYS ACT IN A MANNER CONSISTANT WITH OUR SELF IMAGE

Ovi, we will always act in a manner consistent with our self image; that's why it is also your auto pilot."

"There is one final piece of the jigsaw to put into place and that is the **Master Mind**," said Master Yip.

"Can I ask you something?" Master Yip said to me.

"Of course."

"When you were back in England did you know people who went on a diet?"

"Yes," I replied.

"And people who wanted to stop smoking?" added Master Yip.

"Yes."

"What were these people attempting to do?"

"Err... trying to stop smoking or lose weight? I think."

"Correct," Master Yip said "However there is something that stopping smoking, losing weight, altering your routine or any other variations in habit have in common. Tell me Ovi; what is that?"

I had spent the best part of seven years here at the monastery and I had finally begun to understand how Master Yip's mind worked. He could of course just tell me, but no; he had to make me discover it for myself.

And after some thought I had the answer, "You are talking about a change in behaviour, aren't you?"

"Yes, yes I am Ovi. In order to do something different you have to change your behaviour. I am going to give you an opportunity right now to tell me what the **truth** is. You know Ovi the only law that matters; THE TRUTH! Tell me Ovi.........What is the **truth**?"

I wasn't ready. I didn't know. I was standing there in silence hoping for some kind of epiphany, you know a sudden realisation of the **truth**.

It never came!

"Let me explain the **master mind** to you Ovi. First let me recap; remember this.......*We will always act in a manner consistent with our self image; that's why it is also your auto pilot.*"(This is important.)

"Yes I remember, you kept saying to over and over" I said

"You omitted to ask me one vital and crucial question Ovi. That question is why, why will we always act in a manner consistent with our self-image?"

"I don't know, but I get a feeling that I am about to find out." I said.

"Ovi, if you understand, accept and believe *we will always act in a manner consistent with our self image; that's why it is also your auto pilot.* If you accept that, then you are ready for the next step, the *master mind*."

360 –Degree Power Thoughts

I look forward to the future with confidence and belief.

The
Master
Mind

"Let me tell you Ovi, the master mind has only one job. It is so good at that job it never fails. It has never failed in the history of the universe and it never will. In one way this is your safety valve, it stops you from doing things that you wouldn't normally do, like jumping off a high building or walking out in front of traffic. It also stops you from changing your behaviour. As a child you were told that you need to stop, look and listen when crossing the road; if not, you will get knocked over. You learnt that if you fall or jump from a great height you will come to harm. The master mind will keep you safe. It will also keep you from achieving anything new or different."

Master Yip told me that the master mind has only one job and it is this:-

To keep your behaviour in line with your self-image; your....

Conditioned-auto-pilot-self-image

Both Tommy and Jasmine were amazed by what the Ovi dynasty had discovered about the mind and how that knowledge had the potential power to change **their** lives.

I decided to set the scene and add a comment that I thought was needed.

"You may be wondering what this has to do with success, money and wealth. My answer is everything! The Ovi dynasty's findings that Master Yip was teaching me were not only responsible for the unrivalled success of the Ovi Empire for 900 years; they too were the reason that I had grown my business and had become a member of the elite; the 1% group."

Master Yip was about to fill in the blank jigsaw piece. This would prove to me that I needed to change everything in my life. If I wanted to succeed and make my life a triumph, I would need to put into practice everything Master Yip was teaching. Master Yip drew something on the slate wall that made sense of it all. He then spent the whole night explaining why this one step would bring me closer to uncovering the **truth**.

"Here is the big question Ovi; if you want to change your behaviour what needs to change? If a smoker wants to become a non-smoker or a person on a diet wants to maintain that diet or way of life; what needs to change?"

"Their behaviour?"

"Yes, but what controls behaviour?"

"I don't know"

"Yes you do, we always act in a manner consistent with what..?"

"Our self image? Or our auto pilot?" I answered.

"Yes, so if you want to change your behaviour what do you need to change?"

Talk about a light bulb moment. "Self image, my self- image." I shouted.

"That's where the ***truth*** lies," said Master Yip. "Ovi we need to re-condition our self image. Give it new programs to follow. Listen, since the day you were born you like everyone else has been through a process of conditioning. (**LIFE IS NOT A JOURNEY IT IS A PROCESS**) We see things, we hear things. Taste and smell influence our behaviour, and all that information is stored in our self-image leading us to our auto pilot."

Reality Four and five

The Upholding; Self-talk – Affirmations& Acting to believe!

"Self-talk or the **Upholding** and acting to believe do not work without each other!" I told Tommy and Jasmine. "It's like Morecombe without Wise or Laurel without Hardy. In fact, it's like driving a car without fuel, the car may be in great working order but without the stimulus to make it work it will go nowhere. Tell me have you tried affirmations in the past?"

"Yes and they don't work!" Jasmine said with a disappointing tone.

"Why did they not work?" I added

"Pass, ask me one on sport," Jasmine was positive that it had not worked for her. In truth she was right. There was a reason that it had not worked for her and I'm presuming they haven't worked for you? I continued to tell Tommy and Jasmine

"It was no accident that the Ovi dynasty, the empire had been unstoppable for so long. They followed the process to the letter. Without question **The Upholding; Self-talk – Affirmations & Acting to believe** are by far so superior to anything you have ever done or heard of before, it will blow your mind, oh and change your life.... if you let it"

Master Yip had put this on the slate wall;

Seeds = Language

"Now a seed can be planted by you (self-talk or affirmation) or it can be planted by someone else; anyone. That is called conditioning. ABC"

Weeds = Language

"Now a weed can be planted by you (self-talk or affirmation) or it can be planted by someone else; anyone. That is called conditioning. ABC"

Remember that your current actions, behaviours and choices are not good enough to take you to new heights of achievement

"Ovi listen, the Empire uncovered something that they kept hidden for hundreds of years; an inscription.......

Watch your thoughts, for they become words. Choose your words, for they become actions. Understand your actions, for they become habits. Study your habits, for they will become your character. Develop your character, for it becomes your destiny."

As I sat with Tommy and Jasmine, I was about to reveal the very first action that will set them apart from 99% of other people. This was the very first step to making change happen.

"You see Tommy; Jasmine, the Ovi dynasty found the formula for positive self-talk. Every time you or someone else says something to you it leaves an impression on your self-image and over time that impacts on your behaviour. So it is imperative that you keep your self-talk positive, it is also vital that you spend time with people who are good for you. People who will support you with positive words and actions."

Master Yip wrote on the slate wall;

P + P + P = New Behaviour.

"Think about this for a minute Ovi. What things do we do on a daily, hourly or even minute-by-minute basis? How do we talk to ourselves? What kind of language do we use? What Kind of *Self-Script* do we use? What is a *Self-Script?* I will enlighten you; self-scripts are negative beliefs you have about yourself and of which you remind yourself daily. Self-deprecating remarks that influence your behaviour or beliefs. Everyone does this Ovi; it's just that we don't realise it. You see the *gatekeeper* lets it through to the *holding mind* and then it is embedded into the *conditioned self-image*."

I began to tell Tommy and Jasmine a little more about a self-script. The Ovi dynasty really knew that self-scripts had massive impact on our behaviour

Self-talk or our self -scripts play a vital role in our self -image. Think back to the way we tell ourselves "I can never lose weight." or "I wish I could give up smoking but I know I never will."

Master Yip continued to tell me about the self-script "If we spoke to other people the way we speak to ourselves we would soon make lots of enemies. You are driving down a road looking for a particular house number when you drive past the one you want. How do you talk to yourself? "Stupid" or "Idiot". Imagine saying that to someone else. Calling another person an idiot or stupid would soon lose you lots of friends. However we have no problem in saying it to ourselves."

Master Yip was right, for years I had talked to myself in a very negative way but I didn't realise it; we all do; it's a habit.

The Upholding; Self-talk - Upholdings

It's the repetition of Upholdings that leads to belief. And once that belief becomes a deep conviction, things begin to happen.

So what is an Upholding?

An Upholding is self-talk, ether positive or negative.

What makes an Upholding work?

For an Upholding to work it has to be accepted by the person using it. An Upholding is self- talk; it can be both positive or negative. **This is important**! For an Upholding to be successful it has to follow a specific course of action.

It has to follow the 3 P's formula P + P + P =Changed behaviour.

1   It has to be in the present.

You have to say **'I am'** not **'I will'**. By saying I am sends a message to your self-image and makes an impression on your self-image. **'I am'** means it will happen. **'I will'** means it may or may not happen. If you say **'I will'** it implies it may or may not happen, if you say **'I am'** your subconscious will begin to change your behaviour. (Over time and only if you follow the process

2   It has to be personal.

You can't say an affirmation for someone else. It has to be I am, I am, I am.

3   It has to be positive

If you say **"I am"** you are two thirds to making a positive and lasting impact on yourself. Unfortunately the vast majority of people follow that statement by saying. . . . . . I am an idiot or I am ***** at telling jokes. (Or whatever their limiting belief is.)

They follow it up with a negative and untrue statement about themselves that in turn builds their self image.

The final "P" of an affirmation is that it has to be **Positive**.

I am the best, I am the greatest.

"Tommy listen, and you also Jasmine. This is so important, you and everyone else has failed to use the Upholding (self-talk) correctly. This is the Morecombe; remember we need the Wise to make it work. In this case the Wise is the *Acting to believe."* *(More about that later.)*

"Let's look at each one Ovi and discover why we should make this part of our daily routine," Master Yip said.

Uncovering the slate wall Master Yip presented what the Ovi dynasty called it *The first step*.

Affirmation*; emotional support or encouragement = Upholdings*

"Ovi, an affirmation is a way of talking to yourself; telling yourself that you are good or bad; fat or thin; rich or poor. It is a fuel that your auto-pilot needs to operate. *Your conditioned auto-pilot* will listen to the dominant message that you give it; and then take the appropriate action. So your behaviour will always match your self-image. *The first step* to reconditioning *your conditioned auto-pilot* is to make it believe a different *truth* to the one it currently operates from. Ovi; do you understand?"

"Yes; I need to talk to myself in a better way."

"Ovi; success is a science and you must have the correct conditions to get the results you want. This right here, right now is a scientific process and you must follow that process to the letter for it to work. Overlook, ignore or neglect something and the cake will not be a cake. The process works but you must follow the process to the letter. This of course Ovi is only the *first step*; there are many others you must take."

I turned to Tommy and Jasmine and said "Master Yip made me write down some of the things I said to myself that would make an impact on *my conditioned auto-pilot.* I mean the negative stuff; the harmful words and thoughts that I used without even thinking it."

I handed both Tommy and Jasmine some paper and asked them to jot down some of their negative words and thoughts. I gave them ten minutes.

This is *your* opportunity to do the same. Write down some negative self-talk.

360 –Degree Power Thoughts

I like the person that I have become.

Your negative words and thoughts:-

Here are just some of the things Tommy and Jasmine came up with;

- I'm not good a spelling
- I can't remember jokes
- I don't do maths
- I'm not good with heights
- I am not doing well in my job
- I am not capable enough
- I am lacking so much in life
- I hate my life
- I hate my studies
- I cannot go out alone
- I don't have enough resources
- I could never afford that
- I'm not worthy of that

- I get bored quickly
- I'm fat
- I can't lose weight
- I am a smoker

There were more; but you get the idea.

"My question to you both is; what impact does that kind of language have on your behaviour?"

I could see that by writing this down Jasmine was getting upset; she was noticeably shaken by what she had written down.

"I can't believe I do this to myself," she said "It's exactly like you said earlier; I have been planting weeds and not seeds. No wonder I can't keep to a diet."

"It's not just you Jasmine; 98% of people will sabotage their success without knowing they are doing it. It's automatic!" I continued, "People who want to lose weight or stop smoking constantly tell themselves that they are fat or that they can't lose weight; or a smoker will automatically tell themselves that they are a smoker. Here's the thing; we will always act in a manner consistent with our **conditioned self image.**"

To change our long term behaviour we must change our self image. We must re-condition our auto-pilot our conditioned self-image.

"Have you ever watched an actor trying to portray emotion on the TV; but they are not that good at it?" I asked.

"Yes, there are too many wooden and cardboard actors out there," replied Tommy.

"Let me ask you both; how convincing are they at conveying emotion?"

"Very unconvincing," Jasmine added.

"Here's the thing; and listen very carefully. You have to put emotion and passion into your positive seeds, your words of encouragement to yourself. You cannot be wooden or unconvincing; you must, must, must convince your self-image that you mean what you say! You must act as if you are worthy." **The Upholding; Self-talk – Affirmations & Acting to believe!**

Acting to believe. This is where the most confusion sits. People, you and, I feel uncomfortable pretending to be something we are not. *We are our conditioned self image or auto-*

pilot. Acting like something else will cause conflict, lots of conflict. However the Ovi dynasty had the answer to this, as they did all things. I will reveal that answer shortly.

First let's look at the words we can say to make our behaviour change. The words you are about to discover have been filtered and refined by the Ovi empire to give maximum impact on your conditioned mind. Be very, very careful to follow the process exactly. Some scrolls look like the previous one. They are not. There is a subtle difference between them, so look carefully."

I explained to Tommy and Jasmine that the following scrolls and words were detrimental to the success of their entire future. "You MUST follow this without fail!" I could not stress this enough. The urgency and importance you (yes YOU) put on this will determine your membership to the 2% club, the elite, the select few.

"First get used to the words then I will show you how to **act and believe**" Master Yip told me.

"What follows are five scrolls that you need to conquer Ovi" Master Yip exclaimed. "You need to recite day one at every opportunity. Memorise it and say it over and over again. Say the words in your head when you meditate, feel the words. See the words in your head; you need to believe each and every word. You are now starting to re-program and re-condition your auto-pilot. This will begin the process of changing your behaviour (over a short period of time)"

__Upholding day one__; take three minutes in the morning to look at and **perform** the words written down. Yes I did say **perform** and we will look at that aspect later in this chapter. Three minutes; one hundred and eighty seconds of your life; can you spare that? Keep those words in your consciousness all day, now take three minutes before bed to look at and **perform** the words written down. Six minutes of your life each day, just six minutes for the next 30 days. Are you capable of doing that? I know the answer to that and so do you.

Upholding Day One

I am more than I appear to be

I am worthy

I am open to change

I am open to change

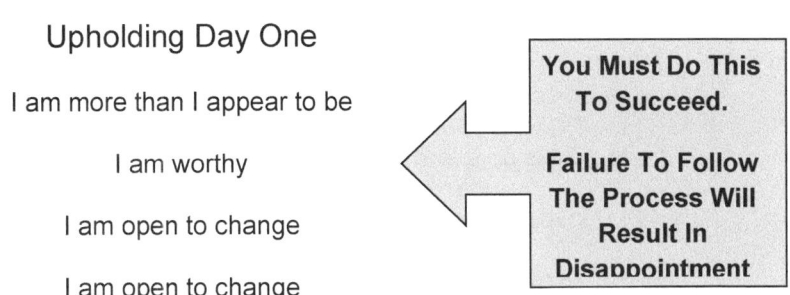

You Must Do This To Succeed.

Failure To Follow The Process Will Result In Disappointment

**Upholding day two**; take three minutes in the morning to look at and **perform** the words written down. Yes I did say **perform** and we will look at that aspect later in this chapter. Three minutes; one hundred and eighty seconds of your life; can you spare that? Keep those words in your consciousness all day, now take three minutes before bed to look at and **perform** the words written down. Six minutes of your life each day, just six minutes for the next 30 days. Are you capable of doing that? I know the answer to that and so do you.

Upholding Day Two

I am worthy of success

If it is to be it is up to me

I love who I am

I am open to change

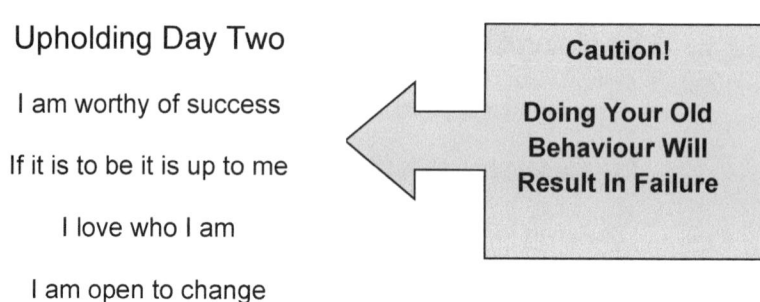

Caution!

Doing Your Old Behaviour Will Result In Failure

Upholding day three; take three minutes in the morning to look at and **perform** the words written down. Yes I did say **perform** and we will look at that aspect later in this chapter. Three minutes; one hundred and eighty seconds of your life; can you spare that? Keep those words in your consciousness all day, now take three minutes before bed to look at and **perform** the words written down. Six minutes of your life each day, just six minutes for the next 30 days. Are you capable of doing that? I know the answer to that and so do you

Day three is different. Look at the words!

Upholding Day Three

I am more than I appear to be

I am worthy

I deserve a better life

I accept success into my life

I am worthy

You Must Do This

Your Master Mind Will Try To Stop You

Just Do It

Upholding day four, take three minutes in the morning to look at and **perform** the words written down. Yes I did say **perform** and we will look at that aspect later in this chapter. Three minutes; one hundred and eighty seconds of your life; can you spare that? Keep those words in your consciousness all day, now take three minutes before bed to look at and **perform** the words written down. Six minutes of your life each day, just six minutes for the next 30 days. Are you capable of doing that? I know the answer to that and so do you.

Upholding Day Four

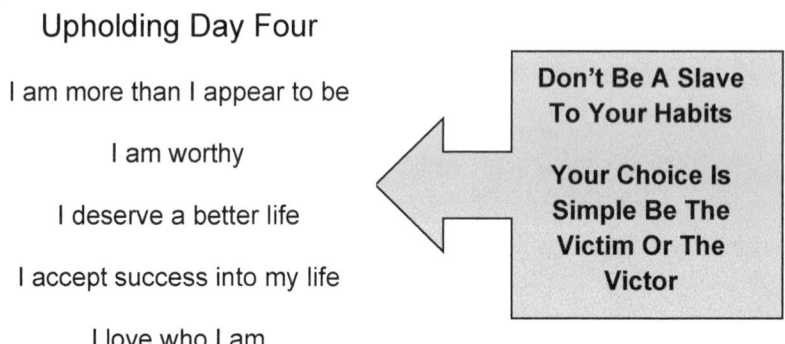

I am more than I appear to be

I am worthy

I deserve a better life

I accept success into my life

I love who I am

Don't Be A Slave To Your Habits

Your Choice Is Simple Be The Victim Or The Victor

Upholding day five; take three minutes in the morning to look at and **perform** the words written down. Yes I did say **perform** and we will look at that aspect later in this chapter. Three minutes; one hundred and eighty seconds of your life; can you spare that? Keep those words in your consciousness all day, now take three minutes before bed to look at and **perform** the words written down. Six minutes of your life each day, just six minutes for the next 30 days. Are you capable of doing that? I know the answer to that and so do you.

Upholding Day Five

I am more than I appear to be

I am worthy

I deserve a better life

I accept success into my life

I am worthy

My life is getting better

I am ready for change

The Only Reality Is The One You See

If It Is To Be It Is Up To Me

You Are In Control

"Ovi, you have completed your first five days of behaviour change, how do you feel?" Master Yip asked. It was usually difficult for me to answer a question like that, but I felt very different.

"I have an inner confidence that I did not have before," came my answer. "Good" came the reply. "I will tell you the process for the next 25 days, listen carefully Ovi, this is important."

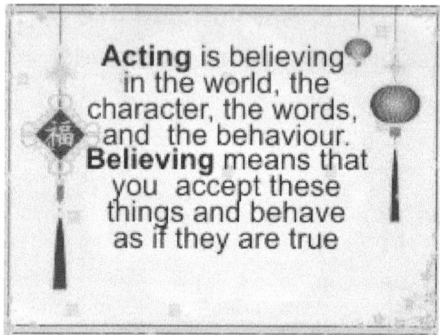

Acting is believing in the world, the character, the words, and the behaviour. **Believing** means that you accept these things and behave as if they are true

This was on the slate wall as I entered the learning space.

"Nine years Ovi and now your learning is just beginning" Master Yip was about to explain the process for real change; how the Upholding can change your conditioned auto-pilot.

"Ovi, this is the part where 99.9999% of people give up or just don't get it, you must understand why this is important. It's the **_why_** that gives it its power.

Unfortunately Ovi you will not find the why within these walls, you will need to look further afield, beyond your comfort zone here."

Both Tommy and Jasmine looked as confused as I did when Master Yip began to explain. It was normal to feel like that.

"You must understand!" I said, "To really make it in life, you know be happy, have more money at the end of the month, to be able to afford the things you want and deserve, you have to do one thing."

"It seems that we have more month at the end of the money recently," Tommy said. "What's the one thing we need to do?"

"Let me tell you how Master Yip made me understand....."

I began to rationalize to Tommy and Jasmine the behaviour that Master Yip displayed and the explanation he gave for doing it. Master Yip was kind and thoughtful, he and the members of the monastery had shown me nothing but compassion and support.

"Ovi, I am going to take you to the lake tomorrow, this will be your toughest test yet. I will need to show a side of my behaviour that you haven't seen.

Remember this. Whatever happens you are safe. No harm will come to you."

360 –Degree Power Thoughts

I focus on positive thoughts.

Morning came and true to his word Master Yip took me to the lake at the very edge of the grounds. "It's time to learn the most important lesson Ovi," he said as he took my arm and we both walked into the water. The clear cold water went from ankle to knee and then to waist. Master Yip kept walking, taking me with him. Now neck high, the water had almost engulfed me. I was beginning to panic, but still Master Yip did not stop.

As I pulled back and turned towards the edge of the great lake Master Yip continued to push me out and then placed his hand on my head forcing me under the water. My arms were flapping like a flag in a gale, I was gasping for air as the cold water filled my mouth. It was a blur and I could feel myself losing the fight to survive. It was like being back in the Indian Ocean clinging onto the plane's wing, then suddenly Master Yip pulled me up above the water. "What do you need Ovi?" he shouted.

Coughing and spluttering I managed to say "Air, I need air."

Master Yip held me under one last time. It was hell, I thought I was going to die right there in the great lake. "What do you want Ovi?"

I was on the verge of passing out but managed to squeak, "Air!"

Master Yip dragged me to the edge of the water and made sure I was OK.

"Sorry Ovi but that was necessary. Let me give you the biggest lesson you have learnt here to date... **Until you want to change and succeed more than you want and need air, you will never make it.** I'm sorry but only a hand full of people both know this and act on it. The Ovi dynasty were the most successful race on planet earth for over 900 years. They knew that without the want to succeed you will not amount to anything"

Walking back to the monastery, Master Yip told me about the journey he wanted me to take. "You will leave this place tomorrow for five days. Here are your instructions."

Master Yip handed me my orders on an old piece of parchment and told me to go and prepare for my travels.

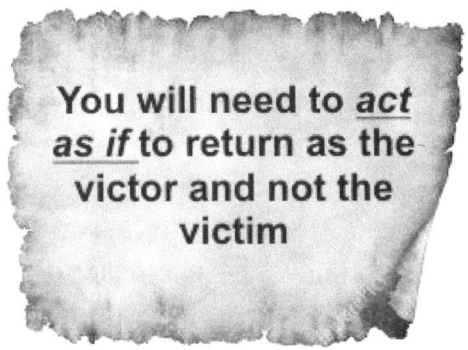

You will need to *act*
as if to return as the
victor and not the
victim

Master Yip had written down the directions and what I needed to do. It transpires that there was a competition in the village fifty miles away. I didn't know that there was a village nearby, the test or competition was on face value simple. Historically, there had been a rivalry between the adjoining villages to see who could plough a field in the fastest time.

And to add to the challenge the plough would be pulled by two horses, two horses!

My only fear was the giant overpowering stature of a horse. I had been thrown off a friend's horse years ago and never wanted to see one again let alone get close to one! How did Master Yip know this was my only fear?

"Ovi, use your Upholding. Now is the time to really tell yourself you can do it. You will need to act as if you are an expert. **Act to believe** Ovi. Despite your fears and the fact you have never done it before you will need to convince yourself that you are an expert in ploughing a field. There are three ways to do this, two of which you know; the Upholding (self-talk) telling yourself that you can do it and that you are the best; and second, acting as if you are the best or **Act to believe**. The third way is called **Pre-Living**; I will show you tonight before your journey."

It was the evening before my journey and Master Yip took me through some more Upholdings; ones that are not in your daily five. I have shared them with you; you need to integrate them into your next 25 days of Upholding.

Master Yip gave me the process of Upholding and how to mix and combine them for maximum effect. I'll let Master Yip explain.

"Remember Ovi, life is a **process** not a journey, **everything** is a process; follow that process and you will achieve your goal. Of course you have to have goals and aims in life; we will teach that here Ovi. The empire called it **Horizons**. Your aim for this task is to be the first to plough the field. The competition starts on Wednesday it will take you two days to get there so you will leave tomorrow. Tonight we will combine the ***Upholding; acting to believe and the pre-living*** to give you all the internal tools you need to return as the victor."

Here are the additional Upholdings Master Yip shared with me. I will show you how to fit them into your existing Upholdings.

360 –Degree Power Thoughts

My self-talk is always positive.

As I sat with Tommy and Jasmine it was clear that they had 100% bought into the concept of Master Yip's teachings. This would prove to be a turning point for them and as a result of their belief; this would put them in the elite if they take PMA – Positive Massive Action on the learning's

Master Yip knew that acting to believe was the most difficult aspect for our conditioned auto-pilot to accept and recognise.

"Because you and everyone else tell themselves they cannot do something repeatedly, time and time again they end up believing it; despite having never attempted to do it. Your mind will automatically decide that you can't do it. *It does not have a reference point.*"

Both Tommy and Jasmine looked puzzled when I said reference point.

"What do you mean by reference point?" Jasmine asked

175

I tried to put it in a way I thought would explain it without adding any complications. You know in a simple way.

"As a very young child or a baby; you attempt to get to your feet and walk. You know it is possible because you see others around you doing it. The thing is you fail, so your first reference point is learning to walk is going to take some time to master. Here is the bottom line, what do most children do after falling?"

"Get back up," Tommy added.

"Yes, but why?" I was hoping both Tommy and Jasmine would discover this for themselves. "Why don't they just give up?"

Five minutes passed before they both gave up.

"Why do we fall?" I asked.

"We don't know," came the reply.

"Why do we fall?" I repeated.

"To get back up?" said Jasmine.

"Close, very close."

"I know this," said Tommy "Why do we fall Bruce?" (in reference to Bruce Wayne). "So we can *learn* to pick ourselves up!"

"Correct, but in addition to that we, as children learn to get back up because we see the benefit of being able to walk."

The next chapter is all about your horizons. Master Yip and the Ovi dynasty realised that having a purpose in life and setting goals was very important. Unfortunately 99% of people are put off from setting goals because deep down they think they cannot achieve them; the Ovi empire re named this Horizons. *You will learn how Pre-Living plays a major part in your horizons.*

Take two positive actions before moving to the next chapter.

1.

It's not who you are underneath...it's what you do that defines you.

2.

Chapter 6

Hand Three

The Last Hand But Not The Truth

Follow Your *Truth* Horizons

"The Truth is the only law that matters"

"Before we move on Ovi," Master Yip instructed "I will show you the process of integrating the additional Upholding into your daily life, listen carefully."

"Here is a reminder of the original 5. You __must__ do this to succeed!"

Day One:

I am more than I appear to be

I am worthy

I am open to change

I am open to change

Day Two:

I am worthy of success

If it is to be it is up to me

If it is to be it is up to me

I love who I am

I love who I am

I am open to change

Day Three:

I am more than I appear to be

I am more than I appear to be

I am worthy. I am worthy

I deserve a better life

I accept success into my life

Day Four:

I am more than I appear to be

If it is to be it is up to me

I am worthy. I am worthy

I deserve a better life

I love who I am

Day Five:

My life is getting better

I love my life

I am ready to change

I am ready to change

I am more than I appear to be

If it is to be it is up to me

I am worthy. I am worthy

There is the truth and then there's perception. Your perception is your truth

Days 1 to 5 you must take time in the morning to reflect on the Upholdings, and also in the evening. Say them at every opportunity. When you are exercising, walking or driving. Say them over and over again.

Now repeat. Master and embed the Upholdings for the next 20 days. Feel them, live them and above all believe them.

Both Tommy and Jasmine had been fascinated by my life in Vietnam, my life in the monastery and the teachings of Master Yip and the Ovi dynasty. We had covered such a vast amount of detail and learning; the thing is there was more to come. In fact we were just touching the surface of the Ovi dynasty teachings, the next step in both the empire's success and my success was to prove fundamental to long term change.

I was preparing for the task Master Yip had set for me. Ploughing the field! Master Yip was about to show me how to really believe I could become the victor. This would bring me one step closer to the **truth**.

That night Master Yip would spend six hours taking me through the **Horizons** process that included in depth teachings on **Pre-living**.

"Now I will share that with you," I told Tommy and Jasmine.

As we sat in the comfort of their home I gave Tommy and Jasmine a challenge, not just any old challenge. The biggest challenge of their lives.

"You must change in order to change," I said "When I return next week to conclude your teachings you must have done your Upholdings everyday without fail, no exceptions and no excuses. When I come back I will help you to unearth the **truth**. However, you have to prove to me that the learning I have brought you over the past two visits have made a difference. I want you to teach me what I have taught you, I want you to take me through the process taught to me by Master Yip. I haven't told you everything, but I need you to teach me what I have taught you so far. I'll be back next week to conclude your leanings and to find out what you have learnt so far..."

I was at home when the call came.

"AJ its Tommy." There seemed to be a tension in his voice, you know nervousness "Sorry to call you but I need to talk to you."

"You sound anxious," I replied.

"I am, well we are. We're not sure what you want us to do before you come later this week. Sorry that's not quite right, we know **what** you want us to do. We are not sure **why**."

That was a great question. Why had I asked Tommy and Jasmine to teach me what I already know? It wasn't for my benefit that was for sure.

"Is Jasmine there Tommy?"

"Yes."

"Put me on speaker please. So you know **what** I need you to do but not **why**, is that right?"

"Yes," came the harmonious reply.

"Tommy, the shed door is open and it's snowing. What are you going to do?"

"Close it."

"You can do better than that Tommy. Yes you close it but what are you doing?"

"I remember" said Jasmine "Taking action, or should I say Positive Massive Action. Am I right?"

"100%" I said. "Now; knowledge is not power, its potential power, without taking action it is useless. Master Yip made me do this part way through my stay at the monastery; this is how he explained it."

"Ovi. To fully understand a thing irrespective, of what that thing is, you must first teach it to others. To put something into action, you know really live it; you must first understand what it is by teaching it to others. That way you become an expert. Listen very carefully Ovi, this is important. *It's the reason why; that gives a belief true power. Understand why*

and you will achieve anything. You will learn more about this in your **horizons**"

"So, I need you to teach me what I already know for your benefit. See you in a couple of days."

And that was that. I was working on a new project, something to keep me busy. If there is one thing I remember from Master Yip it was to never stop, never slow down and keep reaching for new heights. Yes, I had made billions but I had this insatiable and unquenchable appetite to give, give more to people who needed it. I was once someone who needed help. I was broke, alone and desperate. Living on my own and on the edge of ending it all.

Despite it being December, the sky was blue and the sun was out, unfortunately it was minus two and exceptionally bitter. I made my way to see Tommy and Jasmine; I was intrigued to find out what they had learnt and how they would teach me what I already knew.

When I arrived at their home there was an air of excitement. Something was different.

"AJ!" shouted Jasmine "Great to see you, come in."

Something was very different; you could feel it in the air.

"I've got something to tell you," said an excited Tommy, "come in, sit down."

As I sat down both Tommy and Jasmine were eager to talk.

"Before we take you through what we know, I need to tell about what happened on Wednesday. You know Tommy has a shop?" Jasmine said excitedly.

"Yes"

"Well............." Tommy began.

"Let me tell him!" interrupted Jasmine. "So, his shop. We've been trying to build and hire gym equipment for people to use at home instead of going to a gym. 18 months of trying and 18 months of getting nowhere, and before you say anything I know exactly what you are thinking. We have been *trying* and not *doing*. So we decided to take PMA, Tommy went to a networking event on Wednesday. He met this woman who does the same thing in Manchester and wants to expand over here; she wants to buy our equipment, and lots of it."

"That's great news," I said "what have you learnt?"

"We took action by planting seeds; hang on a minute we did everything you have taught us."

"What do you mean" said Tommy.

"Tommy, we have always said 'why us' or 'why can't things go right for a change'. Tommy we have been playing the *victim*, now I see it. We have been a slave to our old habits. Doing what we have always done and blaming everyone but ourselves."

"I get it now!" Tommy added "Taking action... PMA. If it is to be it is up to me! *Two words, five letters both, each begin the same, their ending not so*. You will know when it's time to leave when you have *changed two letters.* We have learnt how to change two letters. But that's not the most important to me... I realised that I have been conditioned to believe things that are not true. ABC."

"Not for me, no, no," added Jasmine "life is a process, not a journey. I still have trouble believing that, but I know it's the truth....." I interrupted.

"*Truth*? Have you found the *truth*?"

There was a long silence.

"Yes!"

"Go on then tell me... What is the **truth**?"

"We fear change?"

"I thought you had it then." I added

"Is that not it?"

"No"

"Am I close?"

"No. I promise you will get it. What else have you learnt?"

"Hang on I'll go and get my notes." Jasmine said

"Hang on" I said "you don't need them, just tell me."

"But I need...."

"No you don't."

"If I am honest AJ it really brought it home for me when you said the friends I have. You were right, I went down to the local pub Tuesday and the same faces were sat in the same place at the same time. Giving each other advice they can ill afford to give." Tommy looked miserable.

"Why so sad?"

"Well, that used to be me."

"Correct. Used to be, it is not you any more is it?"

"No."

"One last thing," Jasmine added, "we have been doing our affirmations and acting like we already have success."

"Great. The proof is that things have improved for you. I told you this really works, it made me financially free and it will do the same for you too. Listen I don't need you to teach me what you have learnt; your actions have proved to me that you are now changing and for the better."

As Jasmine went into the kitchen Tommy spoke softly as if to not let Jasmine hear what he had to say. "AJ; I'm struggling a bit with this, well a lot really."

"What part?"

"All of it really; I feel like I'm not cut out for success."

"That's perfectly normal; I promise you. I spent almost a year with this inner conflict going back and forth. Am I worthy? Can I do it? Master Yip taught me a way to overcome that; and I will teach you how to do the same."

"Really! It's just that Jasmine has really embraced this and is making so much progress. She really is a completely different person. I like it, she is so much more confident and is starting to come up with lots of new ideas for the business. She is even talking about coming to the next networking meeting with me, she would never do that before, I mean never."

"Well that's great for Jasmine. It's also great for you because she will push you to your limits and take you out of your comfort zone. Tommy keep doing your affirmations but really put passion and meaning into them. Listen, what I am about to teach you today will help you to make sense of everything and give you that boost you need," I said as Jasmine came back into the living room.

"Was that a test? Tommy added. "You can't teach anyone; they have to discover it for themselves."

"So you have been listening then," I joked.

As we sat in the living room I had a couple of pieces of paper to give to them both. "Before we move on I just want to remind you of something important. Do you remember this?" I handed them the first piece of paper. "Do you remember this?" I said again. "Yes. Good times are here." Jasmine added. "But we know that's not what it really says."

"Correct. What point was I making?"

After another long silence they both shook their heads.

"I can't remember," Tommy said.

360 –Degree Power Thoughts

I radiate health and prosperity.

"I know. This is a really important lesson," I said and handed them the same piece of paper as before. "Take your time. I have a question after you have looked at it."

"So what part of your learning does this relate to?"

"I know," Jasmine said. "It's how we have been conditioned to see things."

"Excellent. Spot on. It is all about perspective; how we see a situation and how we react to it. When I got back from Vietnam I began to have serious doubts about my ability to be successful, you know, I was now on my own and Master Yip was a distant and far away memory. I began to doubt I could put into action everything I had learnt. But then I remembered what Master Yip said about my inner influence."

"What the hell is inner influence?" Tommy asked.

"It is your inner voice. It's your-self doubt and your inner certainty all in one. It is your flying high confidence and your rock bottom depression. I will let master Yip explain."

"Your inner voice is detrimental to your success Ovi, let me repeat that. *Your inner voice is detrimental to your success Ovi,* so you need to do two things. Number one, *chose your internal words carefully;* you know how you talk to yourself. Number two, *take control of your inner demons*. That voice that tells you you can't, or that you are not worthy. This will be the making or breaking of you. Ovi, you must not fall into your old habits or your old way of doing things. Temptation will be a constant part of your inner world, that inner influence will be there telling you that you are not worthy or that you do not deserve success. Your inner doubt will be your undoing."

"That was a concern of mine so he took me through a process…."

"Ovi; listen carefully. **Act As If (with grace and beauty)** I did not say **Act As (If with arrogance and egotism).** Act as if you are serious about attaining your dream. Walk, talk, and act enthusiastically, creating a single-minded attitude of success toward the results you desire. Our *master mind* will begin to play tricks on us. The Ovi dynasty were way ahead of their time; they were at the cutting edge of psychological science. The scrolls we discovered were detailed and made compelling reading; they gave the clues to the *truth* and made clear why people fell back into their old ways. Would you like to discover what the empire unearthed?"

I didn't need to answer; Master Yip had already begun the next lesson.

"**Behaviour** Ovi; **behaviour**, or lack of it. Let me ask you a question. When you were young and you went to visit family or friends with your parents your mum and dad would say to you 'be on your best behaviour'; but what would that mean? What is best behaviour?"

"Well, to me I would have to be polite, look smart, and not be cheeky. Lots of things really."

"Yes. You need to show best behaviour. Ovi; what is the opposite to best behaviour?"

"That's simple, worst behaviour."

"Logic would say you are right, however that is not the answer I am looking for. There is something more sinister then worst behaviour. If you display worst behaviour you are at least doing something. It may not be the right thing; but you are doing something."

360 –Degree Power Thoughts

I trust myself. I listen to my inner voice.

"What could be worse than worse behaviour?" I asked.

I asked Tommy and Jasmine the same question.

"I don't know, surely its worst behaviour!" Jasmine added.

"I will give you Master Yips answer."

Master Yip was great at explaining; he really was a great teacher.

"Listen Ovi, worst behaviour is bad, but NO BEHAVIOUR is a killer. No behaviour means you do not even try. However, there are three different kinds or types of no behaviour." Master Yip scribed on the slate wall.

Procrastination

Catatonic

Creative Avoidance

"Each one can and will stop you from achieving anything; they really are killers. They work with your conditioned self-image; they work with a partner called auto-pilot. Let me tell you about each one, starting with procrastination. If I asked you to plant seeds in the field and you turn and say 'it looks like rain Master I will wait until it has passed', you are not saying that you won't do it; you will do it but not right now. I ask you to tidy the master hall and you reply 'I will in the morning', you are not refusing to do it, just not now. Procrastination means to put off. This one no behaviour action will destroy all chances of behaviour change; and play into the hands of the auto-pilot."

Handing me an old slate Master Yip said, "Read this."

"Time is an equal opportunity employer. Each human being has exactly the same number of hours and minutes every day. Rich people can't buy more hours. Scientists can't invent new minutes. And you can't save time to spend it on another day. A day can really slip by when you're deliberately avoiding what you're supposed to do."

"You see, the Ovi dynasty discovered that the auto-pilot is pre-programmed to procrastinate." Master Yip whispered, "and because our mind does not have any other reference points, it believes this to be habitual behaviour. Your Life Is Happening Right Now Ovi. Don't let procrastination take over your existence. Be brave and take risks. Your life is happening right now. ...the best possible way to prepare for tomorrow is to concentrate with all your ability, all your enthusiasm, on doing today's work brilliantly today. That is the only possible way you can prepare for the future."

Master Yip made it clear that changing behaviour was not easy; "Auto-pilot will follow the path with least resistance," he repeated "The path of least resistance Ovi. If you choose not to deal with an issue; then you give up your right of control over the issue to your conditioned auto-pilot; and it will select the path of least resistance."

As I sat with Tommy and Jasmine I could see how the words of Master Yip were having a huge impact on them both. "I realised when I came back that we are so scared of being judged that we look for every excuse to procrastinate" I said. "This old Ovi empire proverb made me really stop and think about my life back in the UK. Master Yip sat beside me and told me this was a turning point in my learning here. In fact Master Yip said that if you understand this proverb correctly it will take you to the **truth**; this is what he said. "Lack of confidence, sometimes alternating with unrealistic dreams of heroic success, often leads to procrastination, procrastinators are self-handicappers: rather than risk failure, they prefer to create conditions that make success impossible, a reflex that of course creates a vicious cycle."

I repeated a short extract of that proverb....... *"Procrastinators are self-handicappers: rather than risk failure."*

Master Yip told me to think about that extract and what it could mean.

"Let's talk about the second part of no behaviour Ovi; **catatonic**. This simply means a flat refusal to do anything; not even a hint of procrastination. Just a NO! I ask you to tend the garden Ovi and you say NO. There is no explanation or justification as to why you won't do it; just a flat refusal. The Ovi dynasty wrote this about the state of **catatonic**; *characterized by a marked lack of movement, activity, or expression.*

I had to confess that I felt like this from time to time; in fact in all honesty it was becoming a habit. I had become withdrawn and insular, perhaps entering a state of depression; was this my future? Here living day to day not knowing what the future had in store. Master Yip explained that there were a number of things responsible for this non behaviour; a combination of conditioning factors that have been drilled into us over a period of time causing them to become a habit; stuck in the auto-pilot.

"Ovi; the main cause of a catatonic state is a lack of both vision and goals; the empire called it *Horizon* blindness. You will learn about *horizons* later in your stay here. 99% of the world's population will be happy to accept this into their daily life; that's why they live each day as they lived the last. I will teach you how to escape the clutches of catatonia."

Master Yip was keen to discuss the third non behaviour action. Before he revealed it he reminded me why I decided to stay.

"The Truth is the only law that matters"

The second was;

Your choice is simple, return as the *victim* or stay here until you are ready to return as the *victor*, the *champion* or the *enlightened one*. You will know when it's time to leave when you have *changed two letters*. The *truth* will appear when you are ready.

"Always remember this Ovi, always."

Listening to Master Yip really was an education, the kind you don't get at school.

"Our third non behaviour is **Creative Avoidance;** this is where your auto-pilot finds another gear. You see Ovi, when procrastination and catatonic are not enough your conditioned mind pulls out the big guns. **Creative Avoidance** is the last defence; it is also the most testing of the three. It's called creative avoidance. You basically find every possible way to stop yourself from taking action. The auto-pilots goal of creative avoidance is to protect you from danger. But ironically, many times you are not protecting yourself, but rather stopping yourself from progress, growth and new wins."

Master Yip wanted me to fully understand and appreciate the power of creative avoidance. He asked me to tell him about a friend or family member who had tried to change their behaviour but convinced themselves to revert back to their old behaviour.

I have a friend, Steve. He wants to stop smoking. Just before he was due to fly off on a holiday we had the chance to have a meal the day before. He said that the best way (he believed) to stop smoking was to do it when he had no pressure on him.

Steve worked in sales and had targets to hit; he was under pressure to perform.

On holiday he would be able to relax and take things easy thus eradicating the need to smoke. Plus he would use the patches to help him.

Two weeks after his return we met for coffee. After ten minutes of him telling me how good his holiday was he took a cigarette out of his pocket and began to smoke it. Sensing I was a little confused, he asked me what was wrong. "I was under the impression you were giving up on holiday," I said.

"Mmmmm well this is what happened" Now this has to be the best example of Creative Avoidance I have ever heard. Arriving in America he popped into a chemist to buy the patches he needed. Unfortunately they only had the 28mg, he needed the 32mg. If he took the 28mg it would not have the desired effect. He would be snappy and grumpy; he would have made the holiday a nightmare for his family. Yes that's it he continued smoking so he would not spoil the holiday for the rest of the family. He made a commitment to himself to stop when he came back.

When I questioned him about smoking now he is back he informed me that he needed to use up all the duty free he brought back!

Master Yip smiled and said "Perfect. That's exactly right. We will tell ourselves a very well constructed fake story to justify our existing behaviour. We are so good at it that we 100% believe that the story is true. Someone who smokes but wants to give up will construct a story to justify why they should continue with the old behaviour (smoking). *We will always act in a manner consistent with our self-image our old self; our auto-pilot.* Follow the 30 day self-talk process. Also act *as if* you already have the skills and confidence and avoid the three killers;"

Procrastination

Catatonic

Creative Avoidance

"The Truth is the only law that matters"

Your choice is simple, return as the *victim* or stay here until you are ready to return as the *victor*, the *champion* or the *enlightened one*. You will know when it's time to leave when you have *changed two letters*. The *truth* will appear when you are ready.

"Tommy......Jasmine, there is something you should know. Master Yip called this the *crunch time!* I had been in the monastery for almost 11 years and one thing had been playing on my mind. Something was wrong with what Master Yip was telling me, I didn't know how to approach it. Let me explain..............."

Two words, five letters both, each begin the same, their ending not so. You will know when it's time to leave when you have *changed two letters*. The *truth* will appear when you are ready"

"It's not about the postman is it? Tommy where is that piece of paper with the motto on?"

"The Truth is the only law that matters"

"Your choice is simple, return as the *victim* or stay here until you are ready to return as the *victor*, the *champion* or the *enlightened one*. You will know when it's time to leave when you have **changed two letters**. The **truth** will appear when you are ready"

Two words, five letters both, each begin the same, their ending not so. Two words, five letters both? Two words, five letters both?

I continued, "Victim and victor are both **six** letters not **five**."

"I have been thinking that for ages," shouted Jasmine.

"It took me 11 years to figure this out. It really was **crunch time**." I continued. "Remember when Master Yip took me to the edge of the monastery and walked me into the great lake?"

Both Tommy and Jasmine nodded.

"Master Yip really was showing me the **truth**. I just didn't realise it. Later in the learning space he made me make the connection. The truth is twofold. I knew the first was this"

There is the truth and then there's perception

Your perception is your truth

"The **truth** is **your** truth, not the truth, but your version of it. Mainly, and for the most, part down to your past conditioning. I'll let Master Yip tell you the second part."

360 –Degree Power Thoughts

When I listen to my inner voice, I find the answers I need.

As we sat in the learning space I began to tell Master Yip about a dream I had the previous night.

"I dreamt that I was in hospital surrounded by doctors working franticly to save my life, it felt so real. Everything was blurry, you know fuzzy and dimly lit. It was unclear what was happening. Then I woke up."

Master Yip said nothing for a while, he just sat looking forward.

"It's time Ovi," he said

Before I could say, 'time for what', he stood up and began to write on the chalk wall.

TRUTH = TRU??

"Ovi, two words five letters both. They begin the same but end not so. One word is TRUTH, what is the second?"

I didn't need to think about it, I knew straight away. However the emotion was overwhelming. My eyes began to fill with tears. Master Yip turned and left, but before he disappeared he turned.

"Ovi," he said "If you were drowning and I threw you a life jacket, would you grab it?"

"Yes" I mumbled.

"Ovi, life is short, you deserve to be happy. It is your right, as it is with everyone. Success is an inside job, success is an inside job. We set our own limits. No one else can do that for you. Ask yourself.....is this you at your personal best? Is this achieving everything you ever wanted? Use your time here Ovi to get clarity, decide what you want in life and then make a plan to get there. You will need to be strong Ovi, the world is wrapped in red tape and I couldn't cut through it even with a billion pound sword. Life is like a magic trick, it only works when you get the process right. Ovi, the world outside these monastery walls are a scary place, it's competitive and cut-throat you must have 100% trust in yourself and your abilities."

It was now time to show Tommy and Jasmine how to plan for their future by setting goals. However the Ovi dynasty did not call them goals. To the Empire it was so much more than that. They called them **Horizons**.

"Measurement," I whispered.

"Measurement? What do you mean?" said Jasmine.

"Measurement. You know...." I added.

"Not with you AJ," said Tommy.

"OK, so Tommy you teach boxers how to fight, right?" I said.

"You know I do, you did the same."

"Correct. Each round is three minutes and there are twelve rounds, am I right?"

Looking puzzled Tommy said, "Is this a test?"

"NO"

 "In that case you are right."

"No trick questions Tommy, I promise. What would happen if each round was 4 minutes long and there were fifteen rounds?"

Looking confused Tommy said, "Both fighters would be too tired to continue after round nine. AJ.... is there a point to this?"

Jasmine interrupted. "Tommy! Sorry AJ. What's got into you Tommy? AJ is teaching us how he became ultra rich and all can do is argue and squabble with him, why the attitude?"

Tommy held his head in his hands, "I'm really struggling with this, sorry. I didn't mean anything."

"I've got an idea," I said "Is there anyone who can have Tommy Junior for a couple of nights?"

"Well, my mum said she would love to give us some time together," Jasmine said. "She's itching to have Tommy Junior for a couple of nights."

After arranging the sleepover, I picked up Tommy and Jasmine the following weekend and took them to my favourite remote part of the UK, the Lake District.

I had a cottage on the lake; it reminded me of Vietnam with its sprawling hills and great expanse of water. I gave Tommy and Jasmine a couple of hours to explore and enjoy their new home for the next couple of days.

It was 8am and the winter sun was just rising over the extensive mountain range. I had a task for Tommy and Jasmine and asked them to meet me in the garden. I handed Tommy a saw and a piece of wood, "Tommy, cut that so it fits into the space in the fence."

"OK, where's the tape measure?" he said.

"Why do you need a tape measure?" I questioned.

211

"To measure the gap," came the reply.

"Just guess it," I said

"What? No, I need to know what size to cut the wood."

"Just wing it."

"It won't fit right; it will be too short or too long."

"Ok," I said.....""What am I trying to teach you right now?"

"I know it's not how to build a fence. It's about measurement isn't it?"

"Is it?"

"Tommy," interrupted Jasmine "He's messing with you. Of course it's about measurement."

We sat drinking hot tea overlooking the great lake, watching the steam dance and skip and then disappear into the air. "Tommy, I'm 52 years old and can run 3 mile in 18 minutes, why is that?"

"Because you're a good runner?"

"No! I wanted to. I set it as my life objective to achieve it. I wanted to prove to myself that I could do it, despite my physical limitations. I used Master Yip's horizons map to make it happen, just like I did with my company Ovi Tec. I devised 172 mind maps to make that company what it became, I followed a (THE) process and took action PMA – Positive Massive Action. I measured my journey every step of the way. I wanted to prove to myself.............. I wanted to prove it to myself. Tommy, Jasmine never make your goals something someone else wants you to achieve. Don't do it for the wrong reasons. It has to be for you."

"So how did you do it?" Jasmine said quietly.

"172 mind maps."

"No, the three miles."

"Ha ha. Sorry. In a nut shell........I found my base line. (What I could do it in by running it when I was very unfit.) Then making a decision that I could do it faster. I decided on a target time and put in the hard work. I then mapped out a process that would make it happen. Please remember that life is a process, not a journey."

As we sat taking in the splendour of the lakes I took Tommy and Jasmine back to the monastery and Master Yip.

"Ovi, without direction and purpose in our lives we will always end up where we started. If I said to you to take a walk in the forest, where would you end up?" Master Yip sat and waited for my reply.

"In the forest." I replied with confidence.

"No, stop guessing and think about It."

"So if I took a walk to the forest where would I end up, I repeated. Where would I end up?" Then the penny dropped. "Back here!" I exclaimed.

"Ovi, without direction and purpose in our lives we will always end up where we started. Remember that.........

    I want you to remember this...............................

It's not who we are underneath.................it's what we **_do_** that matters......

All the knowledge in the world is useless and futile unless you take the appropriate action. Do you remember all those years ago when you first arrived and I said **there are many untold truths for you to share when you leave. I want you to tell the world, tell everyone the *truth* "**

"Yes, but I didn't fully understand what it meant. I still don't."

Smiling Master Yip said "It's not who we are underneath.................it's what we **_do_** that matters. First thing you will do when you choose to leave this place is to become ultra successful and thrive by starting your own lucrative company. You will have wealth beyond your wildest dreams. Then and only then, you give back. You will show others what you have learned here and help them to discover the hidden riches they have within their own thoughts."

That was a lot for me to take in, I did understand but couldn't picture myself ultra successful. All that was about to change and fast.

"WHO ARE YOU Ovi?"

"Who am I?" I repeated "You know who I am."

"Yes I do, but do you? Deep down do you really know who you are?"

The truth was I didn't know. I had no idea who I really was. I never took time to find out.

Master Yip added, "Great people who become famous by their own achievement tend to share their success either financially or by sharing knowledge about themselves, WHY, because ***they know exactly who they are***. The only thing you can be sure of is they are human beings and so are you. People are always blaming circumstances for what they are. I do not believe in circumstances. The people who get on in this world are the people who get up and look for the circumstances they want, and if they cannot find them, they make them."

There is one quality that one must possess to win, and that is the knowledge of what one wants, and a burning desire to possess it.

"It's time to find out who you really are Ovi"

360 –Degree Power Thoughts

I see, hear and feel my success growing.

Tommy and Jasmine were engrossed with what I was telling them, it was now time to pay back Master Yip and make good on the second part of my promise to him. The first I had accomplished, I was successful, rich and thriving. I now had to teach Tommy and Jasmine to be the same.

"If there was one thing Master Yip taught me it was this. **Most people never run far enough on their first wind to find out they've got a second. Give your dreams all you've got and you'll be amazed at the energy that comes out of you."** I said to Tommy and Jasmine.

We decided to go inside to the open roaring fire to continue our lesson of self discovery. I had prepared some learning for them both to fill in; I suggest you do the same.

What would you most like to do in life? What career path would you choose if you were **100%guaranteed** to succeed?

_____

_____

_____

_____

_____

_____

_____

Explain **why** you would choose that path?
(Because I want to is not an adequate answer)

_____

_____

_____

_____

_____

_____

_____

_____

_____

_____

What are the three most important things in your life right now? For example; the people around you, the possessions you have, your career? What do you value the most right now?

✓ _____

✓ _____

✓ _____

What drives you to succeed? What is your motivation? Money, status, position in life or happiness and well-being?

✓ _____

✓ _____

✓ _____

✓ _____

✓ _____

Companies and individuals can form a Credo, or Personal Mission Statement. IBM and Microsoft are just a couple of examples of companies that have done that. A Credo or Personal Mission Statement is a summary of the way you will treat others and the commitment level you have to expand your horizons and to commit to excellence.

What would your Personal mission statement be? The key is to keep it short and to the point. (You will find mine at the end of this book)

_____

_____

_____

_____

It's not who you are underneath...it's what you do that defines you.

_____
_____
_____
_____
_____
_____
_____
_____
_____

How would you like to be remembered? What place in history would you like to take?

_____
_____
_____
_____
_____
_____
_____
_____
_____
_____
_____
_____
_____
_____

Question one (What would you most like to do in life? What career path would you choose if you were **100%guaranteed** to succeed?) The answer you gave to that question **is 100% possible**. People are too busy doing their best, in reality they **(you)** need to do what is necessary. There is a subtle difference. The actions people take and the actions people are **capable** of taking are very different. Ask any child what they want to be when they grow up. They know no limits; to a child nothing is impossible!

Now chart your success. Live your vision. Plan how you would like your life to unfold not by doing your best but by doing what is necessary.

What do you need to do in the first 12 months to make this happen? Where do you start? Who do you need to help you?

_____

_____

_____

_____

_____

_____

_____

_____

_____

_____

_____

_____

What is your five-year plan? What actions are you **capable** of taking to **guarantee** its success?

_____

_____

_____

_____

_____

_____

_____

_____

_____

_____

_____

The Extra Mile

Doing more than other people expect, will get you noticed. However, going the extra mile for **you** will bring about a *quantum* **increase i**n your success. The difference between someone who is successful and someone who wants to be, is simple. Successful people do what's **necessary**, not their best. Unsuccessful people fall short of taking the action they are capable of taking.

What's your Extra Mile?

_____
_____
_____
_____
_____
_____
_____
_____
_____
_____
_____
_____
_____
_____
_____
_____
_____
_____

Now that's it, don't you feel as if you have already achieved something? Has it surprised you how long it took you to complete that?

If you put this book away and come back to it in 3 months and then read what you have written you will relate to only 50% of it. Why? Because life never stands still and neither do you.

"Ovi, it's time for your next lesson, **_Horizons_**" Master Yip whispered.

360 –Degree Power Thoughts

I am in charge of my own life. I am taking back my own power.

Alice Meets The Cheshire Cat

The cat only grinned when it saw Alice. It looked good natured she thought, still it had long claws and a great many teeth so she thought it needed to be treated with respect.

"Cheshire puss" she began, rather timidly as she did not know whether it would like the name. The cat grinned a little wider.

Alice continued, "Could you please tell me which way I ought to go from here?"

"That depends a good deal on where you want to go," answered the cat.

"I don't much care where" replied Alice.

"Then it doesn't matter which way you go," said the cat grinning a little more.

"So long as I get somewhere" exclaimed Alice

"Somewhere, somewhere" repeated the cat, "you are sure to get somewhere if you only walk long enough."

21 UFO's and a glass of H2O

21 UFO's

Uniquely

Formed

Outcome

H2O

Horizons 2 Outcomes

Master Yip and I sat in the morning mist, watching the sun rise over the mountains. It really was a wonderful sight.

"Ovi," he whispered "without knowing your horizons your life will not change. Every individual, business and entity must, must, must have something to aim and aspire to; some untrained people call them goals, NO they are much more than that. 21 UFO's Ovi. 21 horizons or outcomes you must achieve; and like life itself there is a successful process you must follow. You will learn that process over the next couple of days. ***It is imperative you follow the process***."

Master Yip went on to tell me about the rule of seven.

"Ovi. seven is a very important number in relation to success. How many days of the week are there?"

"seven," I answered

"And how many wonders of the world?"

Again I answered "seven"

"How many seas are there Ovi?"

"seven"

"There are even seven layers of the skin. Seven is a key number. I will help you to devise twenty one horizons or outcomes. seven short term (zero to eleven months), seven medium term (twelve to thirty-five months) and seven long term (thirty-six months +). Twenty-one in total. Short, medium and long term all have seven different categories that have significant importance."

229

This is what Master Yip wrote on the chalk wall.

Short	Medium	*Long*
Financial	Financial	Financial
Growth	Growth	Growth
Spiritual	Spiritual	Spiritual
Physical	Physical	Physical
Travel	Travel	Travel
Relationship	Relationship	Relationship
Career	Career	Career

I had prepared some sheets for Tommy and Jasmine; you will find them on the following pages. The first step to achieving your horizons is to decide exactly what you want. **How, what, where and when are not important at this point. That will come later. (And the same for why)**

Master Yip had something important to tell me.

"Ovi. This will be difficult for you. You have to decide what you want. This is not easy, **you** have to decide. Only you know what you want. The process behind achieving them is easy, I have the winning combination for that. Making a decision is 99% of achieving your horizons. Remember this always."

As I sat with Tommy and Jasmine I gave them each 7seven sheets of paper, each with an instruction on them. However, I made them sit in different rooms to do this. After all planning your life is a very personal thing. I also wanted to see if there were any common aspirations that they shared. I gave them one hour to finish.

Twenty minutes into the exercise I checked in with both Tommy and Jasmine. Things were not good!

"I'm not in the right mood," Jasmine said.

"I can't concentrate," said a frustrated Tommy.

I knew just what to do.

Getting both of them together I explained **DSD** to them.

Decide State Direct-action

DSD

"Have you ever heard the phrase 'motion creates and changes emotion?'" I asked.

The answer was unanimous "No"

"Changing your physiology means changing your mental state and breaking your negative patterns. Great physiology therefore, leads to great emotions, and that is one of the keys to getting unstuck. Motion, movement, activity or action, you know getting off your ass and doing something."

"What do you mean by physiology?" said Tommy.

"Physiology. Err, movement or changing your physical state. Running, walking or exercise. If you change your physical state it will change your mental state."

I sent both Tommy and Jasmine on a walk around the lake, approximately 3 miles. However, I sent them in different directions so they didn't talk about their goals together. I told them to power walk, you know with meaning and worth.

So the 'S' in DSD stands for **State**. Change your state by exercising or moving your body to change your current state. Only then can you **Decide** what you want and then take **Direct-action**.

When both Tommy and Jasmine back I immediately got them to continue with their horizons.

Now it's your turn. If you need to, change your physiology!

If you are struggling with this I have shared some of Tommy and Jasmines answers on page 208 so have a quick look before you take time to do yours.

Financial

Short Term:

It's not who you are underneath...it's what you do that defines you.

Medium Term

Long Term

It's not who you are underneath...it's what you do that defines you.

Personal Growth

Short Term:

Medium Term

Long Term

It's not who you are underneath...it's what you do that defines you.

Spiritual (Non Religious)

Short Term:

Medium Term

Long Term

Physical (Body, Health Food)

Short Term:

Medium Term

Long Term

Travel (Holidays and Adventure)

Short Term:

Medium Term

Long Term

Relationships

Short Term:

Medium Term

Long Term

It's not who you are underneath...it's what you do that defines you.

Career

Short Term:

Medium Term

Long Term

360 –Degree Power Thoughts

I take care of my body.

As I sat with Tommy and Jasmine I asked them to share some of their answers with me;

Jasmine wrote..........

Short term financial I, want to not get overdrawn in the bank.

Tommy wrote ...

Long term financial to have £250,000 in savings (5 years time)

Jasmine wrote..........

Short term personal growth: read more books

Tommy wrote........

Medium term spiritual......

Meditate each day

I could share everyone they wrote with you but that would not be helpful to you.

Now, for everyone (all 21) there is a formula or process to follow, the process is exactly the same for each one. If you have written each one down; well done. If you haven't, don't be lazy, slothful or plain dumb. **Just do it! Take PMA**

Here is the winning formula or process you need to for each one. I have given you the sheets here to follow the process. Before we do that I will show you how I guided Tommy and Jasmine through the process.

Come to the edge (said life).
We might fall.
Come to the edge (said life).
It's too high!
COME TO THE EDGE!
And they came,
and he pushed,
and they flew.

Let's take a look at Jasmine's horizon from earlier.

Jasmine wrote..........

Short term personal growth: read more books

I have chosen that one because I said the exact same thing to Master Yip when we sat in the learning space. In fact, the best way for you to understand the process around setting your horizons is to let Master Yip explain.

The monastery was a magical place! Surrounded by tranquil sounds and soothing views. Paradise without question. I felt a sense of overwhelming gratitude and a feeling of not being worthy of its splendour.

"Ovi, choose one of your horizons to work with," Master Yip said.

"I would like to read more books," I replied.

"Ovi, that is a statement not a horizon!" shaking his head he continued, "Do you know the difference?"

"Err..."

Interrupting, Master Yip said "One is meaningless; the other guarantees success. You need to fully understand how our complex mind makes sense of language. Let me explain. I need to lose weight."

"No you don't," I interrupted.

"What is the focus in that statement?"

"Weight..?"

"So the focus is weight, not losing weight. Where is the focus in 'I want to stop smoking'?"

"Smoking...?"

"The mind has selective hearing, it's hard wired. We listen to what we want to hear. You have no control over that." Master Yip was intense. "Stop smoking, lose weight, don't be lazy. All negative language Ovi, emphasis on smoking, weight and lazy. You need to re-frame it""

I had never seed Master Yip so intense.

"Ovi, our autopilot is responsible for everything we do. **Everything**. This includes how we listen to what other people say to us and what we say to our selves. We automatically re-frame things and look for the negative outcome. It's an automatic behaviour."

I told Tommy and Jasmine a little true story ....

The little boy's mother was going off to the market. She worried about her son, who was always up to some mischief. She sternly admonished him, "Be good. Don't get into trouble. Don't eat all the chocolate. Don't spill all the milk. Don't throw stones at the cow. Don't fall down the well." The boy had done all of these things on previous market days. Hoping to head off new trouble, she

added, "And don't stuff beans up your nose!" This was a new idea for the boy, who promptly tried it out.

"Planting the negative thought or notion in our head is easy to do," I said to Tommy and Jasmine, "it reminds me of farmer McGinty.

McGinty, a farmer, needed to plough his field before the dry spell set in, but his own plough had broken.

"I know, I'll ask my neighbour, farmer Murphy, to borrow his plough. He's a good man; I'm sure he'll have done his ploughing by now and he'll be glad to lend me his machine."

So McGinty began to walk the three or four fields to Murphy's farm.

After a field of walking, McGinty says to himself, "I hope that Murphy has finished all his own ploughing or he'll not be able to lend me his machine..."

Then after a few more minutes of worrying and walking, McGinty says to himself, "And what if Murphy's plough is old and on its last legs - he'll never be wanting to lend it to me will he?"

And after another field, McGinty says, "Murphy was never a very helpful fellow, I reckon maybe he won't be too keen to lend me his plough even if it's in perfect working order and he's finished all his own ploughing weeks ago...."

As McGinty arrives at Murphy's farm, McGinty is thinking, "That old Murphy can be a mean old fellow. I reckon even if he's got all his ploughing done, and his own machine is sitting there doing nothing, he'll not lend it to me just so watch me go to ruin..."

McGinty walks up Murphy's front path, knocks on the door, and Murphy answers.

"Well good morning Mr McGinty, what can I do for you?" says Murphy.

And McGinty says, with eyes bulging, "You can take your bloody plough, and you can stick it up your bloody arse!"

Back with Master Yip he began to explain the importance of positively re-framing your horizons.

Hand One

Positively Re-Frame your Horizons

"Anything you want to achieve in life needs to be stated in a positive way" Master Yip continued. "It also has to be specific and precise. **I want to lose weight** is nether positive or specific. **I want to stop smoking** is nether positive or specific. **I want to go on holiday** is nether positive or specific. **I will be xxx weight by xxx date. That _is_ positive _and_ specific.**"

I told Tommy and Jasmine to take one of their short term psychical/health goals and re-frame it to be both positive and specific; you need to do the same as we will use it as a template for the remaining 20 horizons.

Physical (Body, Health, Food) Short Term Positive Re-Frame – Write Your Positive Re-Framed Horizon Below;

Master Yip had a major lesson for me. At first I didn't realise just how important it was.

"Ovi, language is so very important. Let me explain."

*Remember that your current actions, behaviours and choices are not good enough to take you to new heights of achievement, you must change!

"Language is a powerful force in everyone's life Ovi. Negative language can be the difference between achieving your life's dreams or never making it out of the starting blocks. **Carpe diem** Ovi, **seize the day**. Make the most of the present rather than dwelling on the past. I sense that something is troubling you Ovi, what's on your mind?"

"I keep waking up."

"Is your bed not to your liking………."

"It's not that kind of waking up Master Yip," I interrupted, and continued "I keep dreaming that I wake up in a hospital surrounded by white coats and there is a high pitched bleeping. Then I see my parents who tell me to go back and say it's not time yet. What's happening to me Mater Yip? What's going on?"

"Remember when you first came here Ovi? I told you you could leave at any time; that is still the case. You are not a prisoner here, you are our guest. You have never spoken about your parents Ovi …"

Master Yip could see my eyes filling with tears, the room became out of focus like looking through a window in a storm. "My parents are dead Master Yip, both of them."

"Were you close to your parents?" Master Yip asked in a low voice.

"Yes"

Master Yip could feel the pain.

"Go, head off into the mountains for a walk Ovi, be here in the learning space at 5am tomorrow. Now go and make a decision to leave this place or stay until the time is right for you to leave. Ovi for what it is worth I believe that your work here is not done, you have so much still to learn. Now go and return in the morning with your decision"

360 –Degree Power Thoughts

I feel re born, free from the past.

As I set off for the mountains I realised that I had already made my decision. I didn't need to think about it. I needed...no, no wanted to stay. I knew exactly where Master Yip would be. I knew I would find him in the reflection space. As I approached, Master Yip was sitting on the floor with his legs crossed looking out at the magnificent views.

"Come, sit Ovi," he said.

I sat. No words were needed.

Its 5am in the learning space and Master Yip had a plan for me. "Follow me Ovi'" he insisted.

We walked to an out building on the edge of the monastery. On the door was the word SPECULO.

As master Yip opened the door he said, "You cannot move forward until you do this next step Ovi."

Inside was unusual, wall to wall mirrors. "This is where you will spend the next six hours Ovi." Master Yip handed me my Upholding scrolls. "I want you to spend the next six hours looking at yourself and to recite and recant your Upholdings. When you look at yourself, take a good look. Remember that the person looking back is your only competition, look deep into their eyes and say your Upholdings. Feel them, believe them and above all accept them as the **truth**."

I spent six hours in a room with only my reflection for company. Humbling, very humbling. Overwhelming in fact. I got to know myself better than I ever have in that short six hour period.

I think Tommy was a little upset with what I was saying, he excused himself and didn't return for about half an hour. It was getting late, but before it was time for bed, I gave both Tommy and Jasmine a copy of the Upholding and sent them to different rooms with a wall mounted mirror.

"Stand in front of the mirror for one hour, look deep into your own eyes and say with feeling and purpose the words written on the paper. Bring them to life. Then get some sleep. It's an early start tomorrow. Tomorrow you will realise your Horizons."

Since returning from Vietnam I had trouble sleeping, I just didn't need it. Before the accident I loved my sleep, I needed my sleep. Now, four hours is more than enough. December is cold in any part of the UK, but in the Lake District it is especially cold. Open and exposed rural landscapes make it particularly bitter. I sat on the patio with the heaters on just looking out at the darkness. I often did this, I find it inspiring.

I was joined by both Tommy and Jasmine who also couldn't sleep. They'd both been crying, I could tell.

I broke the silence, I had to.

"Master Yip told me about the deadly nine. Nine words or phrases that kill success and absolutely destroy anyone achieving their horizons. Would you like to know what they are?" I said softly.

We sat round the heater watching the steam from the cups disappear into the darkness.

Tommy and Jasmine nodded.

"Master Yip told me about the deadly nine. The Ovi Dynasty identified that language is paramount to our success. They identified nine phrases that kill any chance of success. I'll let Master Yip explain."

"Ovi, after hundreds of years of study The Dynasty made the most mind blowing discovery. Words and language have a profound effect on us. Let me explain about the deadly nine. One of the deadly nine used on its own is disastrous, but when you start to combine them, it then becomes catastrophic. The first of the deadly nine is but."

BUT

"Ovi you are guilty of this deadly word. I have heard you. 'Master Yip' you say, 'Master Yip I would like to be rich and successful.....BUT'. You then tell me and yourself all the reasons you cannot do it. Everything that follows BUT is an excuse you tell yourself, why you will fail."

As I sat with Tommy and Jasmine I found myself turning into Master Yip.

"I have listened to both you and Tommy," I turned to Jasmine and continued. "The unconscious negative language you use is constant, I don't mean to be harsh...."

"No, please tell us. It's the only way we will learn, grow and get better." Jasmine said.

"I remember you telling me about the networking event you went to, I also remember you saying things like 'I would like to go BUT I don't have the time' or 'I would like to go BUT I don't think it is for me'. Classic excuse behaviour. We don't know that we do it, we just do. By saying BUT it gives you the option to justify why something hasn't worked. I would like to give up smoking BUT I'm not sure if I can, but I will give it a go. You have now given yourself a get out clause. If you don't manage to do something you can say to yourself 'I told you so'".

"He's right Tommy," Jasmine said

"I know," was the reply.

"The next one is try," I continued

TRY

"Make sure that you finish your homework...."

"I'll TRY," came the response.

Not good enough!

"Make sure you wash the dishes before you come to bed."

"I'll try..."

Master Yip had a saying "There is no TRY. You either do or you do not. There is no TRY. **Carpe diem** Ovi, **seize the day**."

"One thing I learnt from Master Yip was that life is designed to be happy, successful and plentiful. Life is exactly what it is, **_life_**, ambitious, great, meaningful and full of success. Now is the time to embrace it and run with it. Take PMA (Positive Massive Action). Please, please, please never use the word TRY again! It destroys your soul. It gives you an excuse to fail. Here's the thing Tommy, we start to combine the deadly nine with each other, that then compounds the negative effect it has. For example 'I'll TRY to stick to my exercise plan BUT.......Blah Blah Blah (whatever follows is an excuse.)"

"Oh no, no." Jasmine held her head in her hands. "You have just described me, and Tommy. I'm sorry Tommy it's true. That's us."

Tommy, holding Jasmine, agreed "I know, why do we do it, why?"

"Don't be hard on yourself, everyone does it. Everyone who doesn't know about the deadly nine. Let me tell you about the next one...if."

IF

"The word IF is usually followed by the word ONLY. Let me explain. I could be rich IF I ONLY had rich parents. I could have been the next Tiger Woods If ONLY I had put more work in, BUT I just didn't TRY hard enough."

"Wow!" Tommy suddenly said, "You are not going to believe me but I could have been a pro fighter BUT I didn't have the backing of my family. IF ONLY I had a better start in life things would have been different.....that's what I tell myself."

By this time Tommy had stood up and was pacing around and around, he was getting angry, angry at himself.

"Tommy! It's OK, now is the time to put things right," I stood with Tommy until he calmed down a little.

"Sorry AJ, I, I feel like my whole life has been a failure," Tommy said in a low voice.

Jasmine stood and came over to join us, "That so not true, you have Tommy Junior and me. We have a business, a house and we are keeping our heads above water. Yes, we want more in life, that's why AJ has taken time out to help us."

"Let's look at the remainder of the deadly nine, and then it's time to sleep. You have a busy day tomorrow. The next one is hopefully."

HOPEFULLY

I continued. "You ask someone if they would like to come to your birthday party and they say 'HOPEFULLY'. That means no. I hear football managers being interviewed on TV and saying 'HOPEFULLY we will have good game BUT our key defender is out injured, IF ONLY we had a full squad. One thing is for sure we will TRY our best'. One excuse after another."

"The next deadly nine words are actually 3 phrases;" I added

- WOULD HAVE
- COULD HAVE
- SHOULD HAVE

Continuing, "I really COULD HAVE made more out of life. What I SHOULD HAVE done is worked harder at school. I WOULD HAVE more to show for my life, BUT I never had the best upbringing, IF ONLY mum and dad WOULD HAVE paid me more attention. HOPEFULLY I can turn my life around, I will TRY my best to get better."

I stood up in the cold, dark night as my breath disappeared into the darkness. "I hear that every day from people who want my help, if they can't help themselves, then how can I help them?"

Tommy and Jasmine sat looking out into the ibis, I could see their minds working overtime.

"Number 8 on the deadly list is might." I said as I sat down to get some warmth from the heaters.

MIGHT

"I MIGHT stop smoking soon. I need to lose weight, I MIGHT join a slimming club. In reality MIGHT means NO! It means I will continue to lie to myself for as long as I can get away with it. It's a bit like TRY. You are setting yourself up for failure. It's OK though because you have given yourself an excuse to fail so you can justify it to yourself."

I could see that both Tommy and Jasmine were getting tired.

"Let's finish the last one in the morning shall we?" I said standing.

"I think that's best," they said in unison.

I was always a morning person, I loved them. Must be my old army ways? It was 5.30 AM and I was on my out for a run when Tommy appeared.

"Where are you going?" he said with a question in his voice.

"Quick run before breakfast," I answered.

"Can I tag along?"

As we set off Tommy was eager to talk.

"I, well we are so grateful for your help AJ, I mean really grateful."

"I know."

"Why us AJ? Why are you taking the time to do this?"

"I told you, I made a promise to Master Yip to teach the TRUTH."

"You don't understand what I mean. Why us, Jasmine and myself. Why us?"

"Why not? I mean, I see two hard working people who want a better life, I can help you to achieve that."

261

Tommy stopped, "There are so many millions, if not billions of people who could do with your help, you should write a book."

"One day Tommy, one day," I said "come on lets head back."

Sat around the table, I introduced the final of the deadly nine.

"Can't or I can't" I said.

CAN'T

"Did you know the words 'I CANT' is an affirmation? You are telling yourself that you cannot do something. Most, if not all, people will react with a negative response to something new, or something they think they can't do. It's human nature or **_Auto-Pilot Behaviour_**. Babies and young children will try anything you ask of them because they know no different. As we grow and form a conditioned opinion we give up or even refuse to try anything new. This is a conditioned response, you must remember this always. A bit of advice from Master Yip is 'I CAN'T is a destructive, negative and vicious phrase that needs to be buried deep underground and never given the light of day again'."

Positive

3 PMA Steps   See, Hear Feel

Horizon/Outcome

Resources

What Matters

Impact

What Stops You

We moved back outside to continue our Horizon learning.

"It's so important that when you set any Horizon (goal) it must be written in a positive way. 'I will be or I will achieve'. Keep it very positive. There is a powerful process for achieving your Horizons. The best person to explain is Master Yip."

360 –Degree Power Thoughts

I see the best in everyone and help them to succeed.

Master Yip and I were in the learning space, on the slate wall master Yip had drawn the Horizon process, and he called it Horizons 360;

It looked complicated to me, however after Master Yip had explained how it worked, it made perfect sense.

"Ovi, first it has to be positive. We have already spoken about this with the deadly nine. Every, and all Horizons need to be stated positively, this really is important."

I knew when Master Yip was being passionate about teaching and this was one of those times. Master Yip continued.

"Ovi, without direction and purpose, people...you will always repeat old ***auto-pilot behaviour***. Not good.

Not good for future success. The key is to be able to see, hear, feel, taste and touch your Horizon."

Master Yip sat beside me. "Process Ovi, process. Success does not happen all by its self. Everything in life is a process. It's like making tea or baking a cake, it has to follow a process. We work in the fields planting crops. We have to plant at the right time and harvest at the right time. There is a process to nurture the crop to make sure it has the best possible opportunity to thrive. What we do not do is leave it to chance, we have a process of weeding, a process of watering and a process for feeding the crop. Nothing is left to chance, everything is planned. As it should be in life. Step number one has two parts Ovi;

1. Identify the Horizon. What is the Horizon? Write it down.
2. Re-frame or re-phrase it in a positive way.

Step two Ovi is to make it real. You must remember that the mind cannot tell what is real and what is made up. You have to see, hear, feel, smell and taste your goal in your mind's eye. You must make it real. And there is a process for that."

Both Tommy and Jasmine had a Horizon in mind, it was now time to take them through the 'Ovi Dynasty' realisation process. I got them both to relax and to take control of their breathing. Slow controlled deep breath, relaxing each part of their body, a kind of meditation. I was an expert at meditation; Master Yip had made me that way.

"Close your eyes," I said in a low voice. "now the first part of the process is to see your Horizon as if you have already achieved it. If the Horizon is to lose weight, stop smoking, a new car or home, see it in all its glory. Now make that vision super clear, super colourful and vivid. Surround yourself with the vision and step into it. Live it. Now add some sound, listen carefully to every noise, every sound, even the silence. What does it sound like? Now feel it. How does it feel to stop smoking and live a healthy life? How proud do you feel? What does your new car feel like? Touch the seats, steering wheel and interior. How do you feel about achieving this Horizon? Gloat and bask in its glory, feel the feelings of happiness, you deserve them. Now what can you smell? What can you taste? Enjoy the whole experience."

I stayed silent for around two minutes to allow Tommy and Jasmine to enjoy the process.

"Let's move onto the third step" I said as they opened their eyes. "Step three....what matters? What matters about the Horizon? In other words why is it important? Why do you need to achieve this? What really matters?"

I told Tommy and Jasmine how Master Yip made it clear to me.

"Ovi, there is one powerful force behind achieving your Horizons and that is the power of why or what matters about the Horizon? What really matters? Why is it important you achieve this Horizon? I need you to write 10 reasons why you must achieve this Horizon. And one more thing. When, when do you need it by?"

On the slate wall Master Yip wrote;

When?

_____

_____

Why?

    1. .
    2. .
    3. .
    4. .
    5. .
    6. .
    7. .
    8. .
    9. .
    10.

By this time both Tommy and Jasmine were totally absorbed by the whole experience, they had bought into it lock, stock and barrel. I decided it was time for the forth step in the process.

"Step four is to identify what obstacles are in your way. In other words what stops you? What will stop you from achieving your Horizons, from achieving your true destiny? If we can identify, recognise and act on the obstacles we may encounter along the process, we can then plan to overcome them. So now write down what may hinder your progress and a solution to keep you on the right track."

What stops you? (1)

_____

_____

_____

_____

How can you prepare for it?

_____

_____

_____

_____

_____

_____

_____

_____

_____

What stops you? (2)

_____

_____

_____

_____

How can you prepare for it?

_____

_____

_____

_____

_____

_____

_____

What stops you? (3)

It's not who you are underneath...it's what you do that defines you.

_____
_____
_____
_____
_____

How can you prepare for it?

_____
_____
_____
_____
_____
_____
_____
_____

What stops you? (4)

_____
_____
_____
_____
_____

How can you prepare for it?

_____

_____

_____

_____

_____

_____

_____

_____

_____

What stops you? (5)

_____

_____

_____

_____

How can you prepare for it?

_____

_____

_____

_____

_____

———————————————————————
———————————————————————
———————————————————————
———————————————————————

"Ovi," Master Yip said "time to learn step five. Step five in the Horizons process is impact. Who else will this affect? They need to know Ovi, if not they will work against you and not with you. Tell your loved ones about the Horizon and what you need to do to make it happen. They need to buy into it. What are some of the outside influences that could hinder your success? Who needs to know?"

———————————————————————
———————————————————————
———————————————————————
———————————————————————
———————————————————————
———————————————————————
———————————————————————
———————————————————————
———————————————————————
———————————————————————
———————————————————————

_____

_____

"The next step Ovi, is all about resource. Time, money, maybe influence. What do you need to make this happen?"

_____

_____

_____

_____

_____

_____

_____

_____

_____

_____

"The seventh and final step is the most important Ovi! PMA, POSITIVE MASSIVE ACTION. Without action nothing can happen. You need to write down the first 3 steps to make this happen. 3 steps that you **_must_** take within 24 hours;"

It's not who you are underneath...it's what you do that defines you.

1. _____
   _____
   _____
   _____
   _____

2. _____
   _____
   _____
   _____
   _____

3. _____
   _____
   _____
   _____
   _____

As we sat looking out into the hazy distance at the snow covered hills, Tommy and Jasmine put the finishing touches to their first Horizon. We decided to take a break and resume in an hour.

360 –Degree Power Thoughts

The more I help others, the more I help myself.

It's not who you are underneath...it's what you do that defines you.

Chapter 7

Hand Four

The *Truth* – Beyond Attraction

The real secret about the secret

"Do you know how long you have been here Ovi?" Master Yip asked.

"No, well I'm not sure. Why do you ask?"

"I think it is time to reveal the truth about the secret, and I ask because your time here has been an education. Not just for you, but for me also. I will be sad to see you go. Let me tell you about the myth. The myth behind the secret. Ovi, it is imposable to achieve anything including your Horizons without taking action. No amount of visualisation or gratitude will change your life without PMA. Action is the key to any change in life. No action, no change. Visualisation and gratitude can and will work if you understand the process and science behind it. Everything is a scientific process, everything including nature. Mother nature takes action at the right time with the right process behind it. The law of attraction is the process of cause and effect."

Master Yip began to write on the slate wall.

Cause = Effect = Attraction

"Cause and effect is a relationship between events or things, where one is the result of the other or others. This is a combination of action and reaction. Effect is the result of a cause. Your Horizons are the cause, the effect is the result or the attaining of that Horizon. This is where the distinction between just wishing and visualising or taking action gets confusing. I want and need the vision you build in your head to be so strong and powerful that it causes you to take action that results in the effect of you achieving your Horizons."

When I got back from Vietnam, I needed to understand cause, effect and attraction in greater detail. ***The myth of the secret and attraction needs to be replaced with the science of causality and effect.***

I think that was why so many people fell for the myth, it was magical and mystical like believing in the tooth fairy or Santa, you know it's not real but the convoluted, conditioned story behind it makes it real.

The next sentence is why cause and effect is difficult to understand:

A cause is something or someone that creates an effect, brings about a result, has a consequence, or is the reason for a condition. An effect is a result, condition, or consequence brought about by something or someone. A causal chain is a linked sequence of events in which one event leads to the next event and continues up to a final outcome

So let's make it easy to follow.

Cast your mind back to our conditioned self-image and the auto-pilot, we know that language has a massive impact on our behaviour. That is one example of cause and effect. I'll let Master Yip explain:

"Do you like it here in the learning space Ovi?" Master Yip asked. By this time I knew that with each question came an underlying motive.

"Honestly, no," came the answer.

"Why is that?"

"I would prefer to learn outside. I like it better."

From that point on, my learning was all alfresco.

"Do you know why some people behave in a bad way Ovi?"

I was just about to answer, but Master Yip continued.

"Cause and effect. You tell a child that they are naughty (CAUSE) they will act (EFFECT) in a naughty way.

You tell a child that they are good (CAUSE) they will act (EFFECT) in a good way. Words attract behaviour (cause and effect). When a criminal goes to prison they, the authorities, put that prisoner with other likeminded people. Cause and effect. Put a person in prison (cause) they become a better criminal (effect). It's not difficult is it Ovi? A child grows up in a loving home (cause) they become a loving individual (effect). That's why we say like attracts like. Criminals attract criminals because they mix in the same circles. We need to break that cycle of cause and effect."

Back in the lakes with Tommy and Jasmine, we sat in the December sun under the heaters. I had prepared some handouts to make their learning easier.

"Listen," I said as I sat down around the patio table. "The secret to living is giving. That is cause and effect, tell my why?"

There was both a silence and a blank look from the duo.

"Think about it, come on."

"So the secret to living is giving?" Jasmine said with a question in her voice. "Based on what I already know and what you have said, the secret to living is giving because the more you give the more you get? I don't know. Tommy and I give things all the time but nothing seems to come back our way."

"Really?" I answered with a question in my voice. "Listen, Tommy let me ask you a question; do you get a financial reward for teaching at the boxing gym?"

"No, no I don't. I do it because I like it, actually I love seeing the kids grow in confidence and believe in themselves. I don't do it for money."

"Ok," I continued, "if you didn't teach at the gym the chances of us ever meeting would be low if not zero, right?"

"Yes," came the answer.

"So you have put yourself at the heart of the community teaching in your own time for no financial reward. You are giving unconditionally and not expecting anything back. Now listen both of you. Tommy, you were in the right place at the right time when we met, yes?"

A nod came from Tommy. "Yes."

"Ok, so if you decided not to run the gym, you wouldn't be sitting around this table getting free advice from someone who has done well for himself?"

"AJ, I didn't mean that we don't appreciate what you........." I interrupted.

"You are not getting it. I don't want praise or thanks, no. Far from it. This is the most important lesson I will ever give you two. Let me repeat word for word what Jasmine said less than 30 seconds ago......'*Based on what I already know and what you have said, the secret to living is giving because the more you give the more you get? I don't know. Tommy and I give things all the time but nothing seems to come back our way*'. You said nothing seems to come back our way. Let me say that one more time. Nothing seems to come back our way. I promise I am not having a go or being mean. You have just made the mistake that 99.99% of people make. Language is massive, I cannot state that enough, language. What we say to others and more importantly to ourselves is epic, immense and any other words you want to use to describe it. You have just sent a message to your conditioned self-image; you know your auto-pilot. You have just told it that nothing is going to come back and reward you. Cause and effect. Please don't be upset. It's called tough love, I really like you two and your lives will never be the same again. After we have finished here you will be the best version of yourself, and believe me I guarantee you success."

We sat around the table in silence for a short time. "This is crunch time isn't it AJ?" Jasmine said.

"***No, it's just the beginning***," I answered. "Cause and effect or attraction only works if you understand and apply the process behind it, and we are staying right here until you both do!"

Let's make this simple;

Cause	Short Term Effect	Long Term Effect
Stays at home every day and does not meet others.	Poor social skills.	Few friends. Feel lonely. Feel like the world doesn't care about them

"Listen, they have created their own reality," I continued, "that one action of staying home all the time has attracted the feelings of loneliness. Let me give you another example."

Cause	Short Term Effect	Long Term Effect

Takes regular exercise and eats a good diet.	Feels great, looks good no major health problems.	Lives longer without the need for medication. Has good quality of life.

"One action (cause) has a massive impact (effect) on our life. Some people say they have attracted that result. In reality they took action and continued to do that action. Let's take an extreme example."

Cause	Short Term Effect	Long Term Effect
Individual does not work and never has. Relies on benefits.	Little or no money. Poor quality of life. Blames others for their situation.	Living from day to day. No savings. No prospect for a better life.

"That way of life becomes a habit for them, it then becomes conditioned actions and leads to long term auto-pilot behaviour. Their internal and external language becomes negative and reinforces the self-image and auto-pilot behaviour. The law of attraction only exists when and if we take action, true?"

"Yes," Tommy said

"Think about this you two. The law of attraction does not care what you think, it will deliver your thoughts to create your reality. What you think the most, becomes your actions (cause). You will display what you are thinking. The only way to make cause and effect and attraction work for you is to take PMA (Positive Massive Action). I have recently bought a new car and now everywhere I look I see the same car! Why? I'll tell you why, because it is in my dominant thoughts. Thinking about my car (cause) I see the same car everywhere (effect)."

I stood up, "The law of cause and effect works with or without taking action. We have to chose to take the right action. Cause and effect will still work even if we take no action, because whatever we do, we take action. Even if we do not realise it."

I sensed we all needed a break.

"Let's take an hour to meditate and ponder on the enormity of what you have just learnt. Follow me."

I took Tommy and Jasmine to a clearing in the woods, I had built a space for meditation, it had become my go to place when I needed to empty my head and get a clear vision of what I needed to do.

"Stay here and meditate," I said, "I will be back for you."

I left them with one final thought. "The law of cause and effect, some people call it the law of attraction, is based on visualising your outcome or desire and then putting into action a plan. Now really think about this. I have just taken you through a process of Horizons. What are Horizons really?"

A smile came to Jasmines face. "It's the law of cause and effect."

"How so?" I asked

"So, we decided what we wanted. Then visualised it with all the senses, and then put a process behind it. Tommy, it's all making sense now, I have so many Horizons I need to work on. I now know how to achieve what I want. Something has just clicked. Has it clicked with you Tommy?"

Tommy thought for a second. "Yes, but I didn't realise how a simple mind shift could be so powerful."

"Sit, meditate. I will be back soon." I left them to meditate on what had been a revolution for them both.

360 –Degree Power Thoughts

I love myself the way I am.

Positive thinking leads to unquestionable benefits.

I brought Tommy and Jasmine back to the house and presented them with the above statement.

"What is the cause and what is the effect of that statement?" I asked.

Jasmine was really on the ball with this. "Positive thinking is the cause and unquestionable benefits is the effect."

"Well done. I have a couple of things I need you both to do and then we will move on. I want you to write down a cause and then talk about the effect it has. Let me give you an example. Smoking is a cause (action) the effect could be poor quality of life, smelling of smoke all day, permanent damage to health and premature death. So, one cause can have a multitude of effects. Another cause could be the tide coming in and out, (action) the effect (result) could be coastal erosion, over a long period of time the coast line changes. The ocean moves stones and pebbles around having the effect of changing the landscape. One cause can have many effects, write down a cause."

Cause;

It's not who you are underneath...it's what you do that defines you.

_____

_____

_____

_____

_____

_____

"Now the effects;

- .
- .
- .
- .
- .
- .
- .

As we sat in the cold afternoon air, both Tommy and Jasmine really got to grips with the law of cause and effect. I think this final explanation sealed it for them.

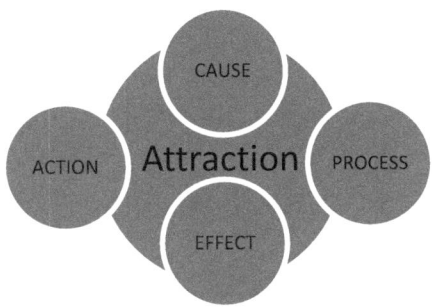

"I need Master Yip to explain this next part," I said as I took a sip from the steaming hot cup filled with green tea.

"Ovi, what is glue?" Master Yip asked.

"Glue? I don't know what it is but I know it holds things together."

"Correct. Your Horizons Ovi are linked to the law of cause and effect, would you agree?"

"Yes"

"I am now going to show you something that the Dynasty tried to keep a secret. They knew that this one action would change the world. They discovered this idea through hundreds of years of trial and error, they called this the glue that bound their Horizons with the law of cause and effect. They called it Time-Zone Horizons. It was a unique way to embed your Horizon deep within your mind and give it a time frame. Sit in the master chair Ovi and close your eyes. I am going to take you through the Time-Zone process. First control and slow your breathing, just like we have practised thousands of times. Now, imagine a line that at one end has your birth and the other continues without ending. The line can go in any direction, there is no right or wrong way to do this. Left to right, right to left. Up, down, diagonal. It does not matter."

I kept it simple, my line went from left to right.

Master Yip continued. "Now on your line I want you to put some Time-Zones on it. For example, in your mind put a symbol to signify your birth. Now we know where it all started. Secondly put a symbol to denote where you are now, but remember to leave lots of room to plot future events that I will ask you to put on there. Now on that line put a symbol to signify one of the first major events you remember. And put the age you were. Do that for other events in your life so far."

360 –Degree Power Thoughts

I create my own reality.

My Time-Zone line was beginning to take shape.

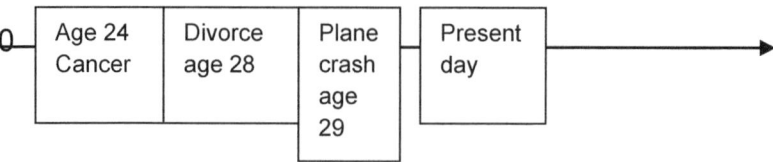

I could have put much more on like, the death of mum and dad but I just didn't want to. I had been through too much at that point, I didn't want to remind myself of all the bad stuff.

"I want you to take one of your goals Ovi, choose the most ambitious one. Write what it is and when you make it happen."

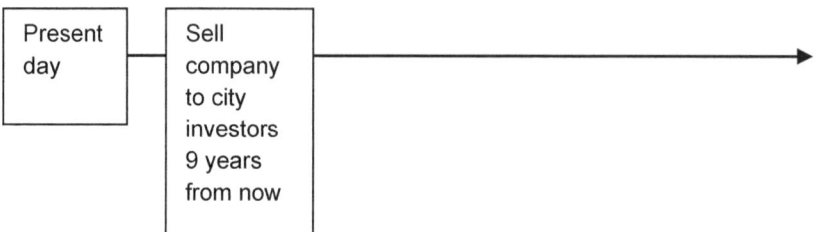

"Ovi, that one Horizon will be your focus for the rest of your time here. I will share with you the inner most secrets from the Dynasty to make that a reality. Meet me here at 6AM tomorrow morning and we will begin work on it. Now is the time for rest."

"Would you like know to what that process was?" I asked Tommy and Jasmine.

"Yes." Was the unanimous answer.

"Over to you Master Yip," I said with a smile.

"Morning Ovi. You are early."

"I couldn't sleep, there was a beeping coming from somewhere in my room last night."

"It will soon be time Ovi."

"Time for what?"

"You will see. All in good time, let's start shall we? What is the first thing you do before you set your Horizons?"

"I need to get into the right state."

"Correct."

"I have just finished a run, like I said, I couldn't sleep. I feel energised."

It's not who you are underneath...it's what you do that defines you.

*Note: Some details have been replaced with xxxxxx due to the nature of AJ's invention. It is currently being used by the military.

"So Ovi, tell me in a positive way what is your major Horizon?"

"Master Yip, it is more than a Horizon. It's my definite major purpose."

"Then tell me."

"The invention I was working on before the crash was to rid the world of terror attacks and the risk of any future world war."

"Now state that in a positive way, war is a negative word, as is terror."

"Ok, to bring peace to the world and to encourage positive behaviour."

"Very good. Now see, hear, feel, smell and taste it"

I immersed myself in a picture perfect environment where my invention would bring about positive changes to the world. It not only helped the military but could save the civilised world from floods, fire and any natural disaster. It became so real that at that time I believed I had already accomplished it. You need to understand that, yes I did sell the company for over two billion pound, the residual income I made from each unit used, was in the region of ten billion pound each year. I did not make that public. Why would I? My true net worth was far beyond what anyone knew.

"Ovi, what matters about your Horizon? Why is it important?"

"I want to......."

Master Yip interrupted, "Don't tell me, that is no good. You must commit it to paper."

- I want to change the world

- Help people to feel safe
- Reduce crime or even stop it
- Stop suffering in the third world
- Give people a feeling of control
- Stop the spread of disease and virus
- I want a better life
- My future family deserve to have what they want
- I can help build safe communities with my wealth
- Live my best life

*The invention of xxx will achieve all of the above and more

"Very good Ovi, now what stops you?"

- Being here
- No money
- Lack of connections
- Skill level
- No business knowledge
- Little or no........

Master Yip interrupted again, "Well done Ovi you have just used the law of cause and effect to fail! Number one, being here will enable you to learn the skills you need to make your Horizon a reality. I see words like lack, no money, no this and no that. Change it Ovi, make it positive."

- Being here will help when I get back to England
- I need to find investment
- I need and want to re-connect with people I know that can help
- Study, I will raise my skill level by learning
- Business knowledge....err...."

For the second time Master Yip interrupted. "Business knowledge Ovi, for the remainder of your time here we will show you how *not* to re-invent the wheel."

At the time I didn't know what that meant but I did know I would find out in due course.

"Well done Ovi, this is important now. I cannot predict the future but I can plan with a high degree of accuracy. I know what will happen when you leave this place. You can and will get caught up in a media frenzy with everyone wanting your story. Do not let this get in the way of your success. Now, what impact will this have on others around you, you need to tell people of your commitment. I have no doubt you will meet someone special and want to be with them. They need to know you will be working on your major life goal 24 hours a day. What impact will this have on you and the people around you Ovi?"

- I need to make time for me, take time to reflect
- Anyone I meet will need to know how important this is to me
- They will need to understand why I am doing this so they can enjoy the process with me

"So, what will you need to make this happen? What resources do you need?"

- Capital
- Time
- Knowledge
- Help
- A place to live
- Money to pay bills
- A part time job to support the bigger picture
- Work ethic

"All valid Ovi, and with my help you will achieve everything. Before the last step Ovi of PMA, Positive Massive Action I need to let you into a secret. Making lists does not work. Turning those lists into a Picture Perfect Road-map will work."

Master Yip continued, "By turning things into a map, a sort of a visual aid, helps to reinforce the message and also helps you to see the bigger picture. What it will also do is help you to really chunk down into lots of detail. This is a visual way to cement a Horizon into your Time - Zone line and make it become real, achievable and realistic. Let me show you a blank one."

Master Yip began to draw on the slate wall that was now positioned in the outside learning space. "The Dynasty called it '360 Mapping'"

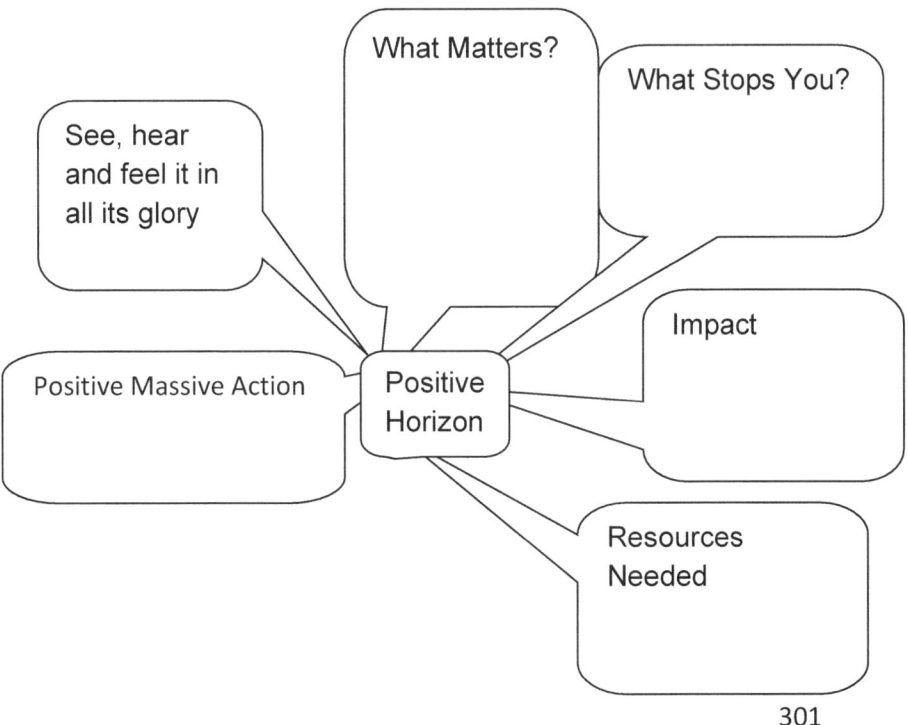

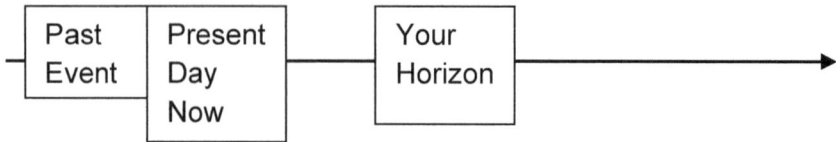

"Let's now look at Positive Massive Action Ovi. What can you do straight away when you get back to England? I mean, without help from anyone else. When you get back and things have calmed down and some form of normality has been realised, what 3 things or actions could you do to begin the process? Let's make that a road map."

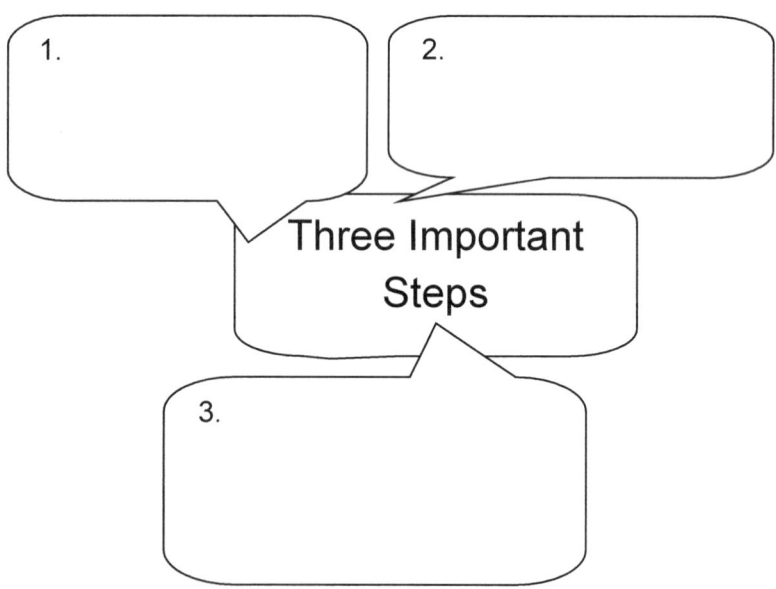

"So, the next step Ovi is to drill down again to get more detail. I want you to write 3 actions (causes) and then what the result (effect) will be."

"Let's put that into your Time-Zone Line."

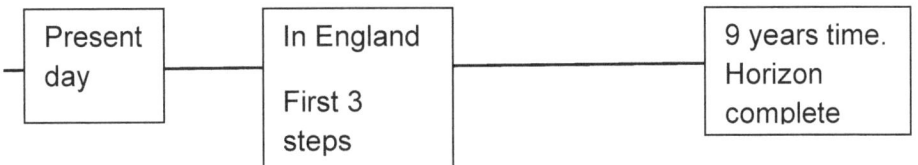

| Present day | In England First 3 steps | 9 years time. Horizon complete |

"Take your Up-Holdings and spend two hours in the mirror space. Remember that you are your only competition. Success Ovi is an inside job. Success is an inside job. What happens between your ears, age, race or sex is not important. Immerse yourself in the knowledge that you are now at the edge of achieving your dreams and Horizons. Ovi....come to the edge."

Master Yip could see the confusion on my face, he continued.

""Come to the edge. We might fall. Come to the edge. It's too high! COME TO THE EDGE! And they came and he pushed and they flew.

Ovi, a bird sitting on a tree is never afraid of the branch breaking, because her trust is not on the branch but on her own wings. Always believe in yourself"

When you do something, you should burn yourself up completely, like a good bonfire, leaving no trace of your old self

Master Yip

.

360 –Degree Power Thoughts

Every experience in my life is an opportunity to grow.

It's not who you are underneath...it's what you do that defines you.

Chapter 8

Hand of Reality

The *Truth* – 12 Years Lost

"Ovi, life is like a magic trick, it only works if you get the process right, that's the problem. People don't know the process, so they just continue to repeat the old program. It's your job to tell the world what you have learnt here and help people to become the best they can be. You must make that promise to me Ovi."

"Of course," I replied.

"Here is the factor that other people will judge you by Ovi. How successful are you? Without any track record they will not believe you or what you teach. You must make OviTec a massive success."

"OviTec? What's that?"

"That Ovi will be your billion pound company. You have spoken about your invention, I can make that a reality, and when you achieve that you will set up the OviTec foundation. The foundation will then fund the World-Wide victory program."

"Victory for who?"

"The people who need it Ovi. All will become clear." Master Yip looked out to the dark ibis. "Remember that success is an inside job. The only limits you have are self imposed...." I had to say something.

"What does that mean?"

"Conditioned old Auto-Pilot behaviour and beliefs. We impose our own limits based on what we think we know. It is not reality. It is however, **our** reality. Not reality to others, but reality to us. The reality of one person is not the reality of another. Your reality before you came here was one of a bankrupted man. Living a life of lack, misery and unhappiness. Do you think everyone in the world was living that reality?"

"No. I know of people who were living a great life."

"What was the difference between you and the others?"

I had enough teaching by Master Yip to know the answer to this. "Mindset," I confidently said.

"In part," came the reply, "there is another factor that we have not yet spoken about Ovi. *Modelling a Successful Process*. You can model two things; a successful company or a successful individual. The main principle and idea behind modelling is that if you completely immerse yourself in the behaviours, strategies, beliefs and process of someone or something that is already successful, you then don't have to re-invent the wheel. You don't have to have the same product or even be in

309

the same industry. Simply look at what they did and make it fit your idea or industry. I will now take you through a process that will give you a detailed road map to make this happen."

"Is that just copying what others do?" I asked.

"In its basic form yes. However, to model a process is to understand what works and what doesn't. Let me ask you Ovi, if you want a better answer what do you need to do?"

I think my stunned silence spoke volumes.

"So, if you want to know the answer to something what must you do?"

"Ask a question?"

"Very good, now if you want a better answer what do you need to do?"

The penny dropped. "Ask a better question!" I exclaimed.

"Correct. Asking the right question at the right time to the right people or person is crucial if not central to learning. In fact Ovi, asking yourself the right questions is vital to your own success, it is vital to help you to put the necessary process in place. People in the 98%. You know, the people who want to get into the top 2% but don't want to put in the work. You were once one of the 98% Ovi. You just didn't know it. The 98% ask 'why me?' or 'I deserve better, why am I never lucky?' Keep asking yourself question like that and you will never be part of the elite, the 2%. Ask a better question. 'What do I need to do to make positive change in my life?' Or 'How can I change my life? What do I need to do?' It's all about asking the right questions!"

Sitting with Tommy and Jasmine, I began to tell them how I prepared for my new company.

"Master Yip and I sat looking out into the impressive landscape, Master Yip told me to make a list of ten people and or companies that I admired. He said this would help with making a success profile and that it would form the base of the process to follow for my company OviTec."

Jasmine sat forward, "Who was on your list AJ?"

"I decided to look at individuals and their companies, so in reality I had a list of twenty. Ten individuals and ten companies. I will share them later with you. What I want you two to do is to start your own list of ten. I'll be back in one hour."

I left them talking about who they would like to model as I went in doors to prepare for an important meeting the following week.

Who would be your top ten?

1. .
2. .
3. .
4. .
5. .
6. .
7. .
8. .
9. .
10. .

Remember about asking questions? Asking the right questions? Volume is not important here, what is important is quality. Let's map it out.

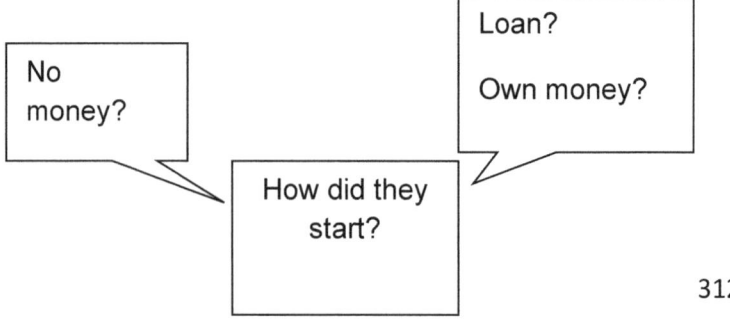

If they took a loan, where did it come from? Bank, investors or family?

Did they fully cost it out?

What about the individual behind the venture? What background did they have?

Who else did they bring into the business to help them? (No man is an island.)

I sat with Tommy and Jasmine and told them about one of my mentors (not Master Yip). Despite this person being a multi Billionaire you won't find him on any rich list, in fact if you met him you wouldn't know his wealth to look at him. This individual started a business with a business partner that eventually sold out to pension fund managers.

He and his partner owe their success to one hundred and seventy two '**road maps**'

Each road map detailed one hundred and seventy two areas that needed to be achieved so the business could flourish. The road map was a detailed visual way to plan and execute a PMA (Positive Massive Action-Plan).

Over a period of months I spent time with both individuals asking question and learning from them. I still keep in touch with them and ask them for advice.

I set Tommy and Jasmine a task for when they got back home later that week.

"So, Tommy, Jasmine I want you to do the following research on your top ten mentoring list;

Buy their autobiography. Read it twice, once as an over view then again to understand it.

Use the web to watch videos and other content to gain an insight into how they think, and their decision making strategies."

It was clear that we needed another weekend together to finish our journey. I wanted to give both Tommy and Jasmine the best possible advantage in life. I had met Tommy Junior and knew how much he meant to the pair of them, they wanted to give him the best start in life.

In addition to making the list of people they wanted to model, I set them two other very important tasks. I say tasks, it was their responsibility to do this. They were now taking action. (It's not who you are underneath......it's what you do that matters.)

Master Yip had set me the exact same responsibility back at the monastery.

"Ovi, I have three tasks for you they are your responsibility to **do**. Everyone thinks they deserve to be successful or deserve a break in life. That's why there are so many disappointed, disillusioned and bitter people in the world. They expect to be great without putting the work in. Three actions you must do. One you can do now, two when you return to England. The first, in preparation for greatness you need to know what your strengths are. What are you good at? You then need to identify what you can improve on, you know things you are not great at but would like to improve on. To finish your first task, what threats will you encounter? This can be anything from external events like war, pandemics or changes in world events. To a great extent things outside your control, but we can still plan for them and have process to make the best of them. It can also be internal factors like fear, doubt and worry. Do this task tonight Ovi, it's your responsibility. The second and third responsibilities you must do when you get back to your home land. The first is to model and replicate the ultra successful. The second is a little strange. When things have settled down and you have come to terms with what has happened to you, I want you to visit some of your old friends. Go for a drink with them, find out what has changed in their life. I think you will be surprised."

I set the same task for Tommy and Jasmine. As I drove them home and arranged to pick them up the following weekend, I reminded them about the importance of taking action. Doing the do, walking the walk and not just talking about it.

It's not who you are underneath......it's what you do that defines you.

360 –Degree Power Thoughts

Everything I touch is a success.

It's not who you are underneath...it's what you do that defines you.

The Beginning of the End

"It's time to listen to the voices Ovi." Master Yip told me. "The voices you hear at night...."

Tommy and Jasmine arrived at my place in the lakes the following week ready for what would be our last get together before I made them an offer they could not refuse. They really had done their home work!

We sat outside again, only this time it was snowing heavily, luckily the canopy was up to the job, as were the patio heaters.

"SIT" said Jasmine"

So I did.

"No, no SIT. Strengths, Improve and Threats. Got them here, would you like to hear them?"

Wow, I hadn't been spoken to like that since school. However I had a hidden agenda.

"Later," I said with a smile. "First I want to know what happened when you went to visit your old friends."

Tommy and Jasmine looked at each other and said at the same time "You first."

"No, I insist" said Tommy

"Well, funny really," Jasmine continued, "school friends never change. No really, I mean it. Live in the same village, never moved. They go to the same place at the same time with the same people. I get it, they like them, they associate with them. You know they have lots in common. Trouble is, they are just as broke as each other but won't admit it. Don't misunderstand me, if that makes them happy then great. It won't make you rich or change your life. That's what I want, to change and give Tommy Junior a better life. I know everyone wants that for their kids but they think feeding them the same old behaviour they got fed will make a difference. All that does, is condition them into a life of just surviving and not really living."

I can't lie, I was really taken back by that little speech.

Tommy didn't say much, but I knew he had something on his mind.

"What was your experience like Tommy?" I casually asked

"Well, mixed really. I mean they seem happy. In fact they are happy so I can't judge them......."

I smiled and said "I hoped this would happen to one of you. If you are happy with your life and it is where you want it to be that's great. This is difficult to explain and even more difficult to understand, but I will endeavour to do it anyway. People are as happy as they make up their minds to be, that's mainly because they never stretch their potential. They don't set meaningful goals (Horizons). They never push the envelope, you know, the comfort zone thing. *People are as happy as they make up their minds to be* conditioned by parents to live within their social class and don't try to reach for something you are not. 99.99% of individuals do not even realise that there is a whole new world outside their conscious awareness. Their conditioned auto-pilot will force them to behave in a way they always have." After a short pause I finished with." And if that is what they want then great for them. I wasn't happy with my life and wanted to change, I just didn't know how to do it."

"I get it now," Tommy said. "If you are happy with your lot then why change?"

"Married with a lack of vision," Jasmine added.

"So the question is, are you ready to change?" I asked.

"We already have," said Tommy

"Oh I know, but if you really want to make a massive difference to your life and more importantly the life of others in your community, I can and want to help. Before you leave here tomorrow I'm going to make you an offer you can't refuse. Now about your SIT exercise, I want you to do something a little different. You have written the answers about yourself, Tommy you have half an hour to do a SIT exercise on Jasmine, and you do the same for Tommy, Jasmine. So you do each other's SIT's, without talking to each other. In fact different rooms, meet back here in half an hour."

We sat watching the snow fall having a bite to eat. I told Tommy and Jasmine I didn't want to know the results of the SIT exercise and, they shouldn't share their findings until a later time. I'll let them know when. I was more interested in how the modelling exercise went. After more than two hours of discussions it was very clear they had modelled and learnt the right lessons.

We will go into great detail about modelling when the time is right.

I was about to introduce Tommy and Jasmine to the most misunderstood aspect of The Truth. People who worship 'Attraction' call it gratitude, but that's a smoke screen. I took Tommy and Jasmine back to my time with Master Yip.

"How do you get really good at something Ovi?"

"By doing?"

"Well done."

It was a strange time at the monastery for me. Every day without exception, Master Yip had spent time with me. It had been five days since I last saw him. I was beginning to worry about him. Five turned into ten.

I woke up the next morning to find Master Yip sat on my balcony looking out at the tranquil landscape, he looked tired and thin. As I approached, he signalled for me to join him.

"I've missed you." I whispered. He didn't answer. He just looked at me. That's when I knew. I had been there myself.

"I don't have long left Ovi," he said.

No words were needed.

360 –Degree Power Thoughts

I can be as successful as I make up my mind to be.

We sat and watched the sunrise. "It's time for your final lesson Ovi. Please don't be sad. You have too much to learn."

What followed was one of the major lessons I had the pleasure of learning with Master Yip.

"When you make a list of things you are grateful for, it does not work. Why is that Ovi?"

"I thought it did work."

"Conditioned Auto-Pilot response. When you make a list and keep adding to it each day, the list becomes so long that you lose interest. It's the reason _why_, that gives anything it truth power. Why is a motivator. Let me prove it to you. What are your top three things you are grateful for Ovi?"

"Health, family and my freedom."

"OK, health, why?"

"Easy. Without my health I have nothing. I mean, without the ability to function correctly I can't earn a living. If I break a leg or become physically unwell I can't work, in fact if I suffer mental illness I can't work. My health is so important to me Master Yip."

As Master Yip began to draw on the chalk board I continued.

325

"I know too many people who have suffered a heart attack or a stroke and never worked again. It affects your quality of life."

"So Ovi, it is fair to say that 'Health' covers a wide range of things, yes?"

"Yes," I nodded

"This is important Ovi. When you make a statement, a positive one, like being grateful for your health, it's too generic and general. We need to be more specific and follow it up with a *why*. Let me give you an example. I am grateful and thankful for my sight because it allows me to look out and appreciate the wonderful colours of the countryside. Or I am grateful and thankful for my ability to walk. It allows me to live a great life."

Positive statement;

I am grateful and thankful for....

Because...

"We could also map it out..."

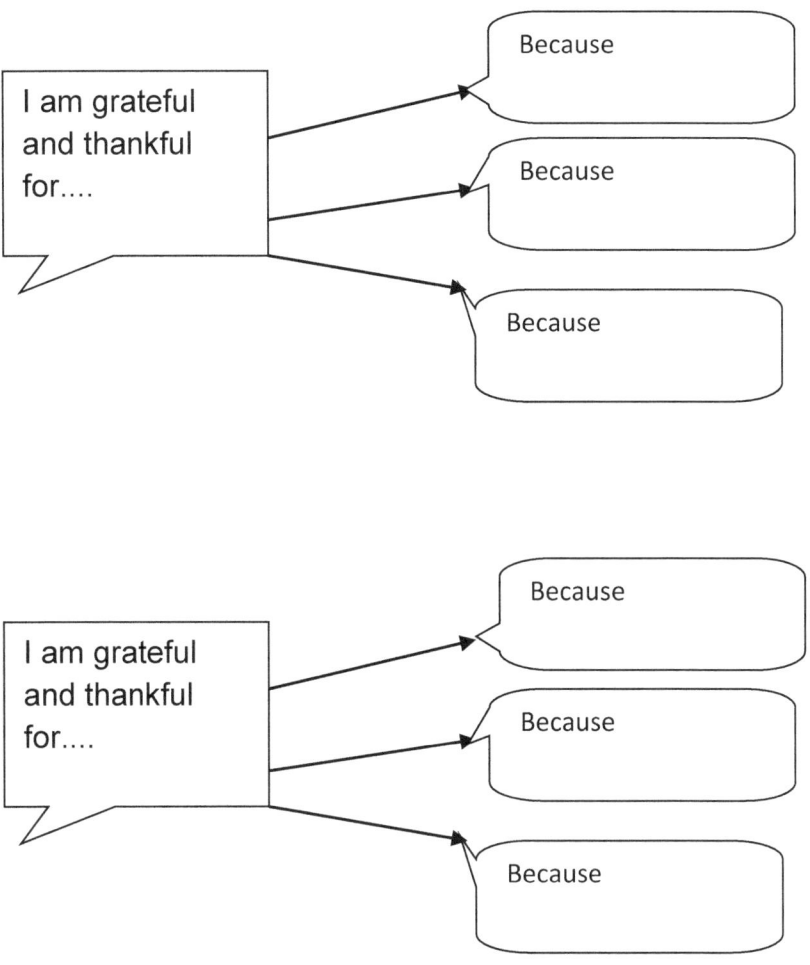

Master Yip needed a break; he was beginning to feel the effects of his illness. He told me to spend the rest of the day reflecting on gratitude and being thankful for the things I have.

The following morning we continued...

"Ovi, gratitude is cause and effect. You think about something you have, it then starts the process of bringing that item or feature to your awareness. You are aware you have it and the things that brings. There is a variety of things that can conjure positive feelings of appreciation or gratitude that may guide people towards meaning and better health."

"Cultivate the habit of being grateful for every good thing that comes to you, and to give thanks continuously. Because all things have contributed to your advancement, you should include all things in your gratitude."

— Master Yip

"Ovi. Gratitude is an emotion similar to appreciation, and positive psychology research has found neurological reasons why so many people can benefit from this general practice of expressing thanks for our lives, even in times of challenge and change. You must first acknowledge the good in one's life. In a state of gratitude, we say yes to life. We affirm that all in all, life is good, and has elements that it makes worth living, and rich in texture. The acknowledgment that we have received something gratifies us, both by its presence and by the effort the giver put into choosing it. Do you understand Ovi?"

"Yes, concentrate on the good and you will bring about more good."

"Ok, but you are thinking about yourself. Gratitude can be given to others without wanting anything back in return. If you give to receive something back, then your intentions are wrong. Gratitude is a selfless act. Its acts are done unconditionally, to show to people that they are appreciated. *A gift that is freely given'* is one way to understand what these acts are like. For example, if someone is sad and you write them a note of appreciation, you are likely not asking for something in return from this person; instead, you are reminding them of their value, and expressing gratitude for their existence. At the moment, you are not waiting for a "return note" from this person."

We sat looking over the lake enjoying what would be our last week together.

"The secret of living Ovi is giving. Giving without expecting anything in return. Showing your gratitude for others and the things you have in life. The secret of living is giving, remember this always. Expressing your thanks can improve your overall sense of well-being. Grateful people are more agreeable, more open, and less anxious. Furthermore Ovi, gratitude is related inversely to depression, and positively to life satisfaction. This is not to say that "depressed people" should simply be more grateful, as depression is a very complicated disease and struggle for millions of people. Instead, perhaps gratitude practices need to be a part of the therapy and treatment for people who struggle with depression."

Back in England with Tommy and Jasmine I was about to give them their last task and then make the offer.

I handed them a couple of sheets of paper and told them to take time to fill them out. (You now do the same.)

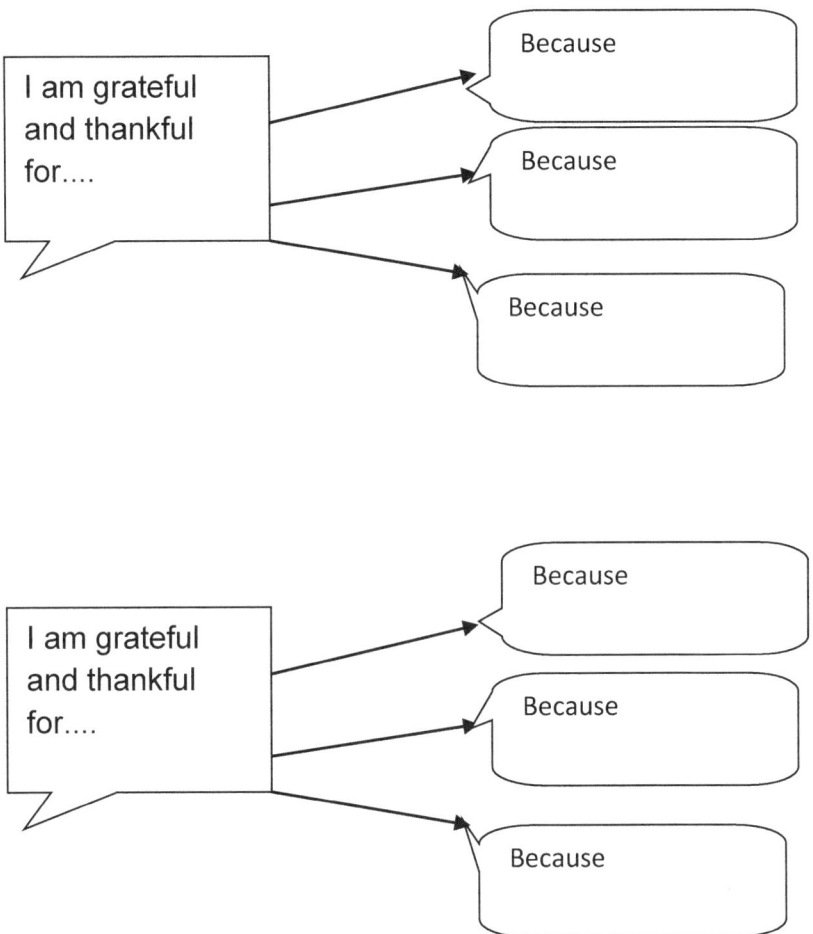

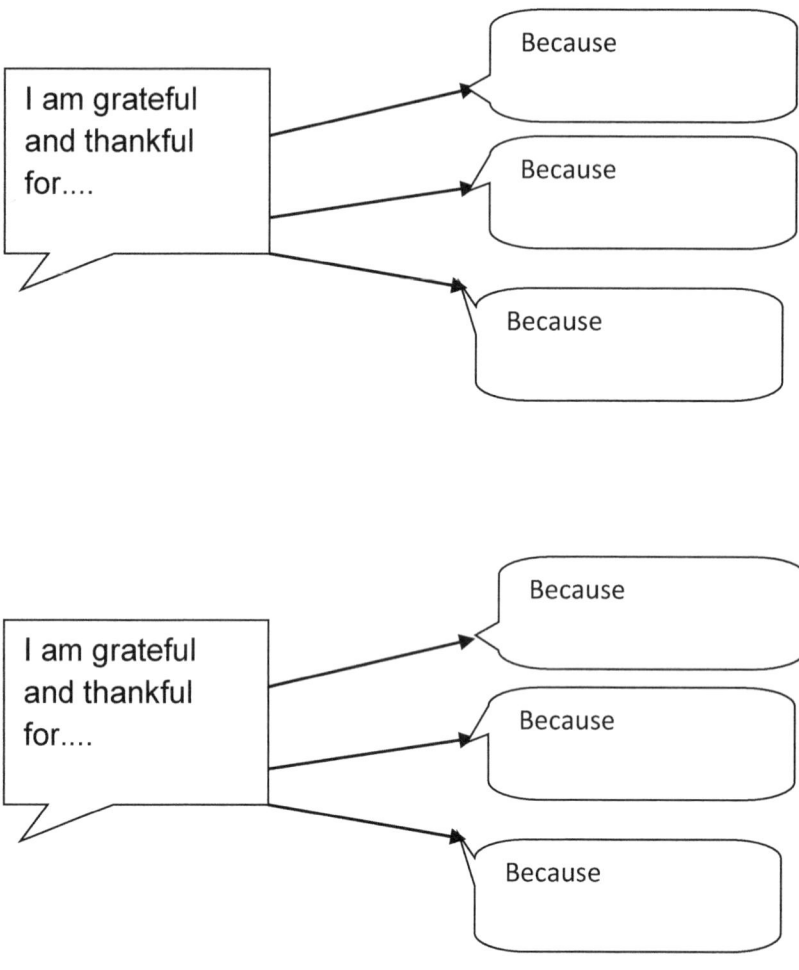

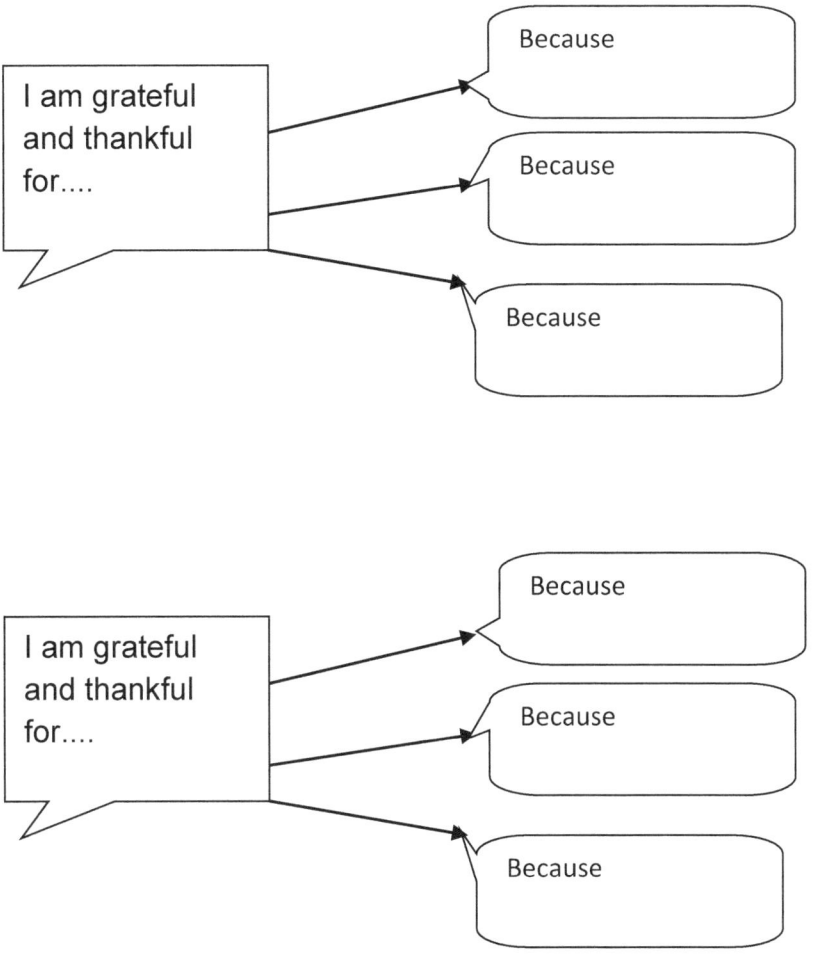

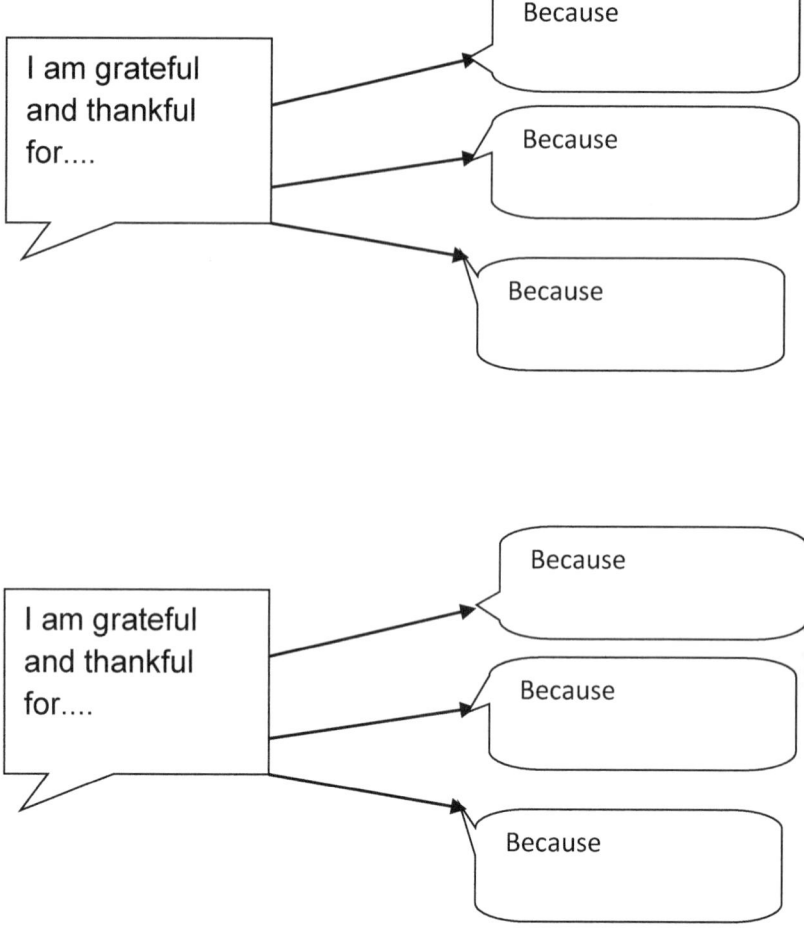

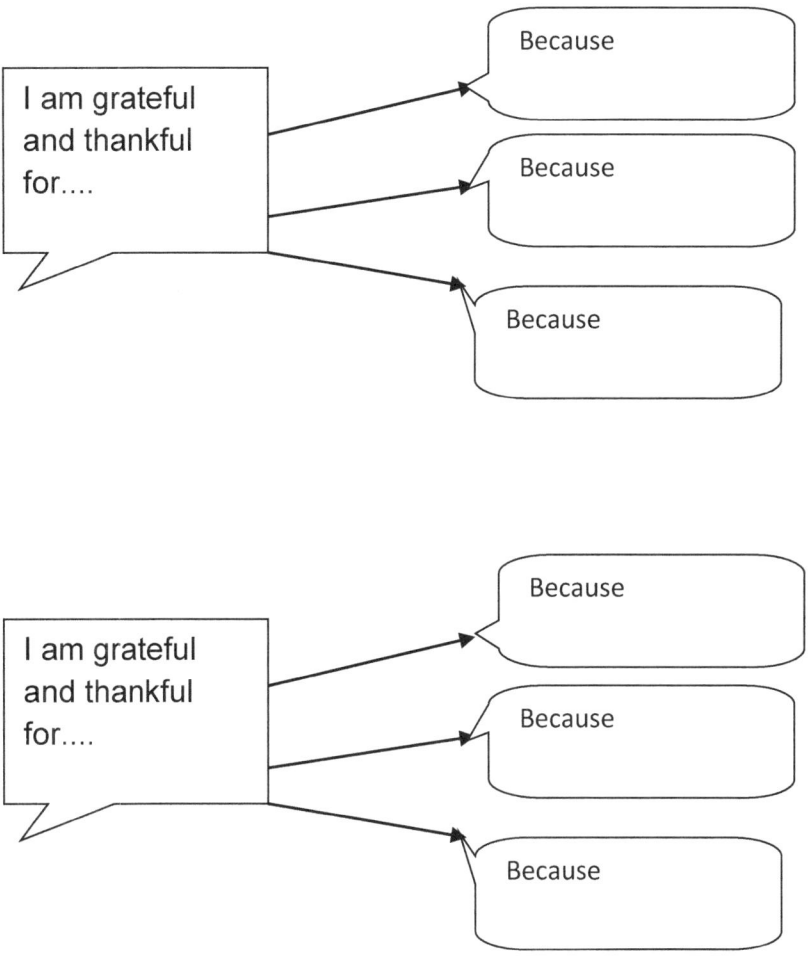

"Showing that you are grateful for what you have means that you will work hard to keep it. Cause and effect. Effect is, you have a nice house; the cause is, working hard and smart to keep it. Setting Horizons means you can plan a process to get better and maybe have a better life with better things. Because the secret of living is giving, the more you have in your life the more you can give to others. So now this brings me to helping you two. Before I do, I need to tell you how I got back from Vietnam."

I moved closer to Tommy and Jasmine. "This is very difficult for me to talk about, everything I have told you about Master Yip has been...well..."

"Are you OK AJ?" Jasmine asked.

"Let me take you back to my last week at the Monastery."

"It's time to listen to the voices Ovi," Master Yip told me, "The voices you hear at night...."

360 –Degree Power Thoughts

I now take care of my mind and body.

Master Yip became so ill that he became bedbound, it was obvious the end was in sight. He called for me, 3 AM I was woken up by the elders. "He's asking for you. Come with us."

Master Yip was holding a small round object, as I sat beside him he whispered "It's time for you to leave this place Ovi." He put the object in my hand and said "Tell everyone about your time here Ovi, tell the world. Your time is now, take it. Now go. They are calling for you."

All I could see were white coats, a blur of faces looking at me.

"Hello, can you hear me? Hello."

There was a blinding flash of vivid white light, then I began to see. I shouted for Master Yip but everyone around me didn't seem to hear me. It was clear I was in hospital. I had been for 12 years.

The look on Tommy and Jasmine's face was priceless. "What.... you mean all your learning was not real, I don't understand," Jasmine said

"I don't get it," Tommy added, continuing "You've made Billions from what you have learnt from Master Yip, was there ever a Master Yip?"

"Yes...and no. We all have a Master Yip within us, we just don't know it or we don't believe it." I said

"Sorry AJ, you became one of the richest people in the UK because of what? I'm really struggling here...."

I had to interrupt, "You are struggling. How do you think I felt? I lost 12 years of my life. I had to learn to live again. I came back to England to find my only family member had passed away, I had no one. The airline was found to be at fault and awarded me a payout. However that's not the end of it. After around five weeks my belongings arrived at my home, you know the ones I lost in the crash. Among the clothes, personal effects and tat was a small round object, a coin. No ordinary coin though, it had an inscription on it. It said;

"It's not who you are underneath...it's what you do that matters"

On the other side it said

"Master Yip"

339

...I had never seen that coin before. It wasn't with me when I left England. They found me clutching it in my hand as I clung on for life. Someone put it in my personal belongings for safe keeping."

I put the coin on the table. "Look!"

I continued, "It took me 18 months to come to terms with what had happened. I kept having dreams every single night. The learning never stopped. Master Yip visited most nights until one night it just ended. That's when I made a decision to do something that would define me. I set up OviTec."

We sat watching the crisp white snow fall in silence. Darkness surrounded us from every direction. I felt alive, safe and truly reborn.

"It's time for you to step up," I said "I have something for you. Your life is about to change...."

What both Tommy and Jasmine did not realise was I paid attention to everything they said from the very beginning. Over our first meal together when I first met them, Jasmine made a throw away comment. She said that both Tommy and herself would love to help people who were not as fortunate as them.

"We have a passion for helping people who are not as fortunate as us. That's why Tommy runs the gym. It's not just a gym, we feed people, buy them things they need and really look after them."

When I asked where the money comes from Jasmine replied, "From us. To be honest AJ we do struggle for money but it's nothing compared to what some people are experiencing. From parents not being able to feed their kids, to stabbings in the local area, it's gone mad! We try to give the young ones a sense of pride and self-worth but it's hard, really hard."

I could see Jasmine getting emotional. "Listen, I have something that can help. Help the local community here and anywhere in the UK. Master Yip made me promise to teach the Truth. Teach it to the world. He also told me to set up the 'foundation', a charity to help educate families and ... well anyone who wants to get out of a rut. I should know, I have been down to the very bottom and then sunk even lower. I want you and Tommy to run it from the gym. I will give you every resource you need to modernise and refit the gym, new equipment and everything needed to be the hub of the community. Let's make it work here and then take the model across the UK. What do you say?"

"I don't know what to say......."

"Just say yes........."

TBC

With thanks to Master Yip.

All illustrations by Sylvia Senior

With special thanks Rosie Hellewell, for her eye to detail.

In memory of;

George & June Radford

Mary & Brian Senior

Master Yip

Gone but never forgotten

www.lastingchange.uk

It's not who you are underneath...it's what you do that defines you.

More Power Thoughts;

Life loves me!

All is well in my world. Everything is working out for my highest good. Out of this situation only good will come. I am safe!

It's only a thought, and a thought can be changed.

The point of power is always in the present moment.

Every thought we think is creating our future.

I am in the process of positive change.

I am comfortable looking in the mirror, saying, "I love you, I really love you."

It is safe to look within.

I forgive myself and set myself free.

As I say yes to life, life says yes to me.

I now go beyond other people's fears and limitations.

I am Divinely guided and protected at all times.

I claim my power and move beyond all limitations.

I trust the process of life.

I am deeply fulfilled by all that I do.

We are all family, and the planet is our home.

As I forgive myself, it becomes easier to forgive others.

I am willing to let go.

Deep at the centre of my being is an infinite well of love.

I prosper wherever I turn.

I welcome miracles into my life.

Whatever I need to know is revealed to me at exactly the right time.

I am loved, and I am at peace.

My happy thoughts help create my healthy body.

Life supports me in every possible way.

My day begins and ends with gratitude.

I listen with love to my body's messages.

The past is over.

Only good can come to me.

I am beautiful, and everybody loves me.

Everyone I encounter today has my best interests at heart.

I always work with and for wonderful people. I love my job.

Filling my mind with pleasant thoughts is the quickest road to health.

I am healthy, whole, and complete.

I am at home in my body.

I devote a portion of my time to helping others. It is good for my own health.

I am greeted by love wherever I go.

Wellness is the natural state of my body. I am in perfect health.

I am pain free and totally in sync with life.

I am very thankful for all the love in my life. I find it everywhere.

I know that old, negative patterns no longer limit me. I let them go with ease.

In the infinity of life where I am, all is perfect, whole, and complete.

I trust my intuition. I am willing to listen to that still, small voice within.

I am willing to ask for help when I need it.

I forgive myself for not being perfect.

I honour who I am.

I attract only healthy relationships. I am always treated well.

I do not have to prove myself to anyone.

I come from the loving space of my heart, and I know that love opens all doors.

I am in harmony with nature.

It's not who you are underneath...it's what you do that defines you.

.